The 20 British Prime Ministers
of the 20th century

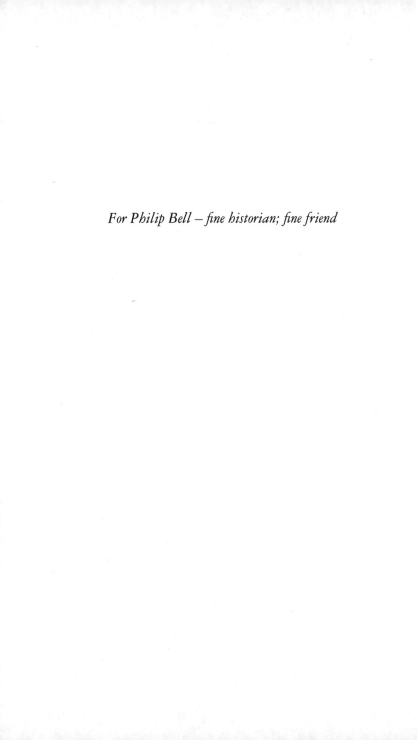

For Philip Bell – fine historian; fine friend

Douglas-Home

DAVID DUTTON

HAUS PUBLISHING · LONDON

First published in Great Britain in 2006 by
Haus Publishing Limited
26 Cadogan Court
Draycott Avenue
London SW3 3BX

www.hauspublishing.co.uk

The moral right of the author has been asserted

A CIP catalogue record for this book is available from the British Library

ISBN 1-904950-67-1

Designed by BrillDesign
Typeset in Garamond 3 by MacGuru Ltd
info@macguru.org.uk

Printed and bound by Graphicom, Vicenza

Front cover: John Holder

Contents

Preface

If Boswell, the biographer of Dr Johnson, was right to assert that no-one should write the life of a man who had not eaten, drunk and lived in social intercourse with him, then I am immediately disqualified from the task I have attempted of writing a brief biography of Alec Douglas-Home. But I can at least claim that our paths crossed on two occasions, each of which left me with lasting impressions of his strengths and weaknesses. As a young boy I accompanied my mother and brother to the celebrated meeting in the Rag Market, near Birmingham's Bull Ring, during the general election campaign of 1964, at which the then Prime Minister was howled down by rowdy Labour activists. It was my political initiation. Forty-two years on, my recollection is hazy. I remember large crowds, stink bombs and a politician who simply could not cope. Though reluctant to admit it within a staunchly Conservative family, I became (briefly) a Harold Wilson supporter, albeit one too young to vote. Many years later, with my political understanding hopefully enhanced, I interviewed the then Lord Home in connection with a biography I was writing of Sir John Simon. We spent an afternoon together at the House of Lords. Home was charming, courteous and helpful. He struck me as a genuinely nice man, though I also sensed his political skills as soon as my questioning entered areas he wished to leave concealed.

I have a number of debts which I must acknowledge. My first must be to the large number of scholars whose work I have plundered in the preparation of my own book. I am grateful to Francis Beckett for inviting me to write this biography; to Ralph White and Thelma Williams for casting a critical eye over the text; to Peggy Rider for typing my manuscript at near record speed; and to Paula Mills for help with the final typescript. But these expressions of thanks should not be taken to imply any attempt to share responsibility for remaining errors of commission and omission, for which I take sole responsibility.

Part One

THE LIFE

Chapter 1: Early Life and Career (1903–55)

Alec Home's life encompassed almost the entire 20th century. He was born – Alexander Frederick Douglas-Home – on 2 July 1903, two and a half years after the death of Queen Victoria in the premiership of Arthur Balfour. He died, over 92 years later, on 9 October 1995 with John Major the current tenant of 10 Downing Street. His place of birth – 28 South Street, near Park Lane in Mayfair – reflected no more than the contemporary belief of the Scottish aristocracy that an address in the capital on a new arrival's birth certificate would offer the most advantageous start in life. For the Douglas-Homes were a family whose roots were firmly set in the Borders. Alec's grandfather was the 12th Earl of Home, the owner of 100,000 acres and two baronial mansions. His father, Charles Douglas-Home, was the heir to that title and its accoutrements. Family life alternated between the Hirsel near Coldstream and Douglas Castle, 30 miles to the south of Glasgow, a migration determined largely by the ritualistic calendar of the shooting season. Alec's parents' own home was Springhill House, a six-bedroomed Georgian dwelling a few miles from the Hirsel. The Lordship of Home in the Scottish peerage dated back to the 15th century, while the sixth Lord had been created an earl by James VI of Scotland soon after the union of the crowns in 1603. The family had become seriously rich as a result of marriage into the Douglas family in the 1830s and the inheritance this brought over 20 years later. By the 1880s the royalties from the coal deposits beneath the family lands in Lanarkshire were bringing in around £60,000 per annum. Life at the Hirsel under Alec's grandfather reflected this affluence with an indoor staff of around 40 and a further 30 or so outdoor workers helping to manage the immediate estate.

It was once usual to suggest that Alec Douglas-Home came from a class which was born to serve. If by this was meant an innate disposition towards a life in national politics, recent family history did not bear it out. His great-grandfather, the 11th Earl, had worked his way through the Foreign Office to become an under-secretary in the administration headed by the Duke of Wellington, but he was the only one of Douglas-Home's predecessors to have served as a government minister. More recently, his father had stood for Parliament, reluctantly and unsuccessfully, as Conservative candidate in the constituency of Berwick and East Lothian, but that proved to be the limit of his political aspirations. Typically, the Douglas-Homes were prominent and industrious in local affairs, allowing them to spend the majority of their time in the countryside which they loved. Douglas-Home would later recall that his father was *a countryman, a naturalist, and he kept us out of doors all the time. He was quite a good bird man.*[1] Though his own life in politics would necessitate a more or less permanent move to the south, his spiritual commitment remained north of the border and, whenever public life became oppressive, he would seek a day or two on those estates whose *healing balm ... never failed to cure and bring content.*[2]

The young Douglas-Home grew up in this environment, a quiet, reserved child, little given to boisterous behaviour and showing few signs of any particular distinction – 'a very ordinary little boy' as his mother later recalled.[3] His education was typical for one of his social background and, in its detail, common to the male members of the Douglas-Home family. In September 1913, shortly after his tenth birthday, he took up residence at Ludgrove Preparatory School in New Barnet. Here, the academic instruction and, more particularly, the sports coaching that he received equipped him for the move to Eton in 1917. There, despite the impact of the First World War on the availability of teaching staff, his intellectual curiosity was developed. But sport, especially cricket, remained his passion. The resident coach, George Hirst, nurtured his talent and, by the early 1920s, he had become an accomplished all-rounder in the school's First Eleven. His appearance in the Eton-Harrow match in 1922 would afford him the distinction of being the only British Prime Minister who had played first-class cricket. An innings of 66 in 90 minutes indicated that he had 'the courage of his convictions and could hook and pull the turning ball effectively'.[4] Though he took no part in Eton's newly formed Political Society, he was elected President of 'Pop', the school's prefectorial oligarchy charged with its unique combination of social privileges and disciplinary powers over the younger boys. If the recollection of his contemporary, Cyril Connolly, is to be believed, Douglas-Home was now making a mark as the 'kind of graceful, tolerant, sleepy boy who is showered with all the laurels, who is liked by the masters and admired by the boys without any apparent exertion on his part, without experiencing the ill-effects of success himself or arousing the pangs of envy in others'. In the 18th century, concluded Connolly, such a man would have become Prime Minister before he was 30.[5]

Douglas-Home himself would later suggest that Eton had empowered him with independence, tolerance, self-discipline, responsibility, reticence and a sense of fun, together with a recognition that power and authority should always be exercised with restraint. At all events, he went up to Christ Church, Oxford to read history in October 1922. Contemporaries, or near contemporaries, included Alan Lennox-Boyd, the future Cabinet minister, Roger Makins, who would become a diplomat of distinction, and A L Rowse, the Cornish historian, left-wing activist and Shakespearean scholar. The pattern of his life showed little change with study taking a poor second place to cricket, and political activity nowhere to be seen. The Oxford Union, the nursery of so many aspiring politicians, held no attraction for him. Only his membership of the so-called Aspidistra Society, whose members were committed to the immediate destruction of such plants, indicated a late flowering of boyish humour. Despite some suggestion that his academic performance may have been impaired by minor ailments, his third-class honours degree scarcely indicated intellectual distinction. As a 'gentleman', he had perhaps, according to the conventional wisdom of the day, secured his appropriate reward.

By the time that Douglas-Home came down from Oxford his position and prospects had significantly changed. With the death of his grandfather in 1918, his father had become 13th Earl of Home, while Douglas-Home himself, as the eldest of five sons, was now next in line to the earldom and entitled to use the courtesy title of Lord Dunglass (as he will be referred to in the rest of this section). Death duties obliged the new earl to sell most of the contents of Douglas Castle together with parts of the Scottish estate and a London home in Grosvenor Square. To speak in terms of straitened circumstances would be an unwarranted exaggeration, but for the Douglas-Homes, like many aristocratic families, the war had been a watershed. Dunglass fully understood his obligations in terms of managing the estate and preparing for the inheritance that would one day be his but, before settling down, he was determined to see something of the world. His sporting talents led to an invitation, readily accepted, to tour South America with the MCC in the company of such distinguished players as Pelham 'Plum' Warner and G O 'Gubby' Allen. According to Warner, 'as a batsman he is quick on his feet and hits hard, is a very fair medium right-handed bowler, and an excellent silly-point'.[6] By 1927 he was back in Scotland and undertaking the sort of local duties thought to be appropriate for one of his standing – work with the local Boys Brigades, Burns' Clubs and Literary Societies. But life as a country gentleman had its obvious limitations and *I was always rather discontented with this role and felt it wasn't going to be enough.*[7]

> *I was always rather discontented with this role and felt it wasn't going to be enough.*
>
> DOUGLAS-HOME

Slowly and, in view of his earlier indifference, unexpectedly, his mind turned towards a career in politics. The catalyst for this change of heart was almost certainly the unemployment, much of it long-term, which scarred the Lanarkshire towns and villages with which he was familiar and for which the government of the day had no obvious answer. He drifted naturally but not inevitably towards the Conservatives, notwithstanding descent through his maternal grandmother from the Whig Earl Grey, famed for his role in the Great Reform Act of 1832. Like Anthony Eden, under whom he would first occupy a Cabinet seat, Dunglass was greatly influenced by the now largely forgotten Tory MP, Noel Skelton. The latter's work *Constructive Conservatism* first appeared as a series of articles in *The Spectator* in 1923 and served as an inspiration for a generation of young Conservatives. The greatest of all social truths, he argued, was that 'the success and stability of a civilisation depends upon the widest possible extension amongst its citizens of the private ownership of property'.[8] To Skelton's goal of a 'property-owning democracy' were added ideas of industrial democracy, share options for workers and industrial co-partnership. Imbued with such advanced thoughts, Dunglass found himself standing as Conservative – or, as the party continued to be styled in Scotland, Unionist – candidate at Coatbridge and Airdrie in the general election of 1929. It was a necessary, but doomed, initiation onto the political battlefield. Both the nature of the constituency and the drift of political opinion after nearly five years of less than inspirational Tory government pointed towards a Labour victory and Dunglass finished more than 7,000 votes behind the successful socialist candidate.

Fortune, however, was on his side. Within months of his defeat at the polls, Dunglass was chosen to become prospective parliamentary candidate for neighbouring Lanark. Though by no means a safe Tory seat, it was certainly more promising than Coatbridge and Airdrie, and Dunglass soon threw himself into the task of nursing his new constituency. To be successful he needed to court the mining vote and it was probably with a view to broadening his appeal that, contrary to the official party line, he gave some support to Lord Beaverbrook's campaign for Empire Free Trade. With a minority Labour government in office, the present parliament was unlikely to run its full course and, following the formation in August 1931 of an all-party National Government to deal with the country's worsening economic crisis, a general election was called for 27 October. In normal times Dunglass's victory would have been far from assured. But these were not normal times. The Labour government was widely seen to have run away from the crisis which had precipitated its downfall and the electorate responded in unprecedented numbers to endorse the National Government. In Lanark the Labour candidate, J Gibson, was probably unwise to publicise the support he enjoyed from the celebrated left-wing Clydeside MPs. Dunglass was elected to Parliament with a comfortable majority of nearly 9,000 votes.

Among a sea of more than 550 government supporters, many of them elected to the Commons for the first time, it would have been easy for Dunglass to have languished indefinitely in backbench obscurity. Not only was there a surfeit of Conservative aspirants for ministerial office, but the claims of the National Labour and Liberal National components of the government could also not be ignored. But Dunglass was invited by Noel Skelton, now a junior minister at the Scottish Office, to act as an unofficial assistant parliamentary secretary. Such a position did not preclude contributions to Commons debates and Dunglass made his maiden speech in support of the government's Import Duties Bill on 15 February 1932. Invoking the words of Lloyd George in his support, he endorsed

> **William Maxwell Aitken** (Lord Beaverbrook) was born in Canada in 1879. Making a fortune on the Stock Exchange, he moved to England in 1910 to pursue a political career, accepting a peerage from Lloyd George in 1917. He acquired the *Daily Express* in 1916 and became one of the major British 'press barons' of the 20th century, using his papers to champion his cause of imperial free trade. During the Second World War Churchill appointed him Minister of Aircraft Production, where he is credited with securing substantial increases in output, and Minister of Supply. He died in 1964.

the formal ending of free trade with the argument that new problems demanded new remedies from a new generation of politicians. Meanwhile Skelton made use of Dunglass's local understanding to help him with a range of matters of Scottish administration. In these early days of his parliamentary career Dunglass was already displaying that consensual and non-confrontational approach which would become his hallmark and, somewhat to his own surprise, he developed an incongruous friendship with the fiery left-winger Jimmy Maxton, with whom he shared a love of cricket. The threats of the Labour left, he once declared, were *only the theoretical ramblings of genial idealists.*[9]

Dunglass stayed with Skelton until the general election of 1935. Much of his work was of an entirely routine nature but represented the necessary apprenticeship of any aspiring politician. After the landslide of 1931 some swing back to Labour was almost inevitable and Dunglass's majority fell by 2,000 when the country went to the polls in November. Safely returned to Westminster, he now became Parliamentary Private Secretary to Lieutenant-Colonel Anthony Muirhead, Parliamentary Secretary at the Ministry of Labour. In absolute terms it was a humble appointment, but it gave him some opportunity to extend his knowledge on the industrial front. Dunglass was clearly making a good impression. By February 1936 he was on the move again, singled out now to become PPS to the Chancellor of the Exchequer, Neville Chamberlain. The appointment was even more significant than it appeared. By this time it was widely understood that Stanley Baldwin was looking to retire from the premiership. Apart from Chamberlain, no successor was even under consideration. Within the foreseeable future Dunglass could expect to take up a position near the very heart of the British governmental machine. But it is important to define what that position was. As Chamberlain's PPS Dunglass was in no sense a policy maker, nor even usually a policy adviser. Neither did he become, in the true meaning of the term, the future premier's confidant. This latter was less a reflection of any shortcomings on Dunglass's part than a function of Chamberlain's reluctance to take anyone outside his close family circle fully into his confidence. Apart from routine administrative duties, it was Dunglass's role to be Chamberlain's eyes and ears in the House of Commons, to act as a sort of liaison officer with the parliamentary party, transmitting and receiving information, and to keep his master informed of the mood on the government's back benches. It was no easy task. Chamberlain proved to be one of the least 'clubbable' occupants of 10 Downing Street. *I liked him*, Dunglass recalled. *I think he liked me. But if one went in at the end of the day for a chat or gossip, he would be inclined to ask 'What do you want?' He was a very difficult man to get to know.*[10] Trying to get Chamberlain to socialise with the backbench members of the House of Commons upon whom his political fate would one day depend was an unrewarding assignment. *He made no effort to put himself across and no one could really do it for him.*[11]

Chamberlain moved effortlessly to the premiership following Baldwin's retirement in May 1937, taking Dunglass with him. The latter quickly became an indispensable member of what a later generation would refer to as the Prime Minister's 'kitchen cabinet'. When Chamberlain was approached by the senior Tory backbencher, Leo Amery, it was Dunglass who advised the premier that he carried little weight in the party and that his claims to office could be safely ignored. 'Alec Dunglass and I have woven a net around the PM whom we love and admire and want to protect from interfering, unimportant noodles', noted a fellow Chamberlain loyalist in May 1939.[12] Chamberlain, like Dunglass, had spent his entire political career to date associated with ministries on the home front. Almost certainly, he would have wished his time at Number 10 to mark the culmination of a distinguished career in domestic administration. But the prevailing political agenda determined otherwise. Chamberlain's unhappy premiership would be completely dominated by the worsening international situation and the government's ill-fated response to it – the policy of appeasement. Dunglass would be damaged by association. In later years when Chamberlain's reputation lay in tatters, damned as the pre-eminent 'Guilty Man' among those who had brought the country to the brink of invasion and disaster in the spring of 1940, Dunglass too would be remembered as a 'Man of Munich'. Though he had no role at the policy-making level, it is only fair to record that Dunglass did not in any way dissent from the main lines of the Prime Minister's foreign policy. To his credit, moreover, he would not later jump on to the populist bandwagon, overcrowded by those who sought to condemn Chamberlain whom once they had praised. Dunglass always believed that Chamberlain had been right to explore every possible avenue to preserve the peace, even though with hindsight he came to appreciate that the Prime Minister had been wrong to persuade himself that, *where neither concessions nor persuasion nor power had changed Hitler's mind, his own reasonable approach could do so*.[13] Even after the Nazi occupation of Prague in March 1939 had opened many eyes to the unappeasable nature of Hitler's ambition, Dunglass still hoped that Poland could be induced to make concessions over Danzig to avoid the sort of confrontation that would drag Britain into war.

His position made him witness to some of the most dramatic moments in British history, not least the scene in the House of Commons on 28 September 1938 as Chamberlain seemed to be preparing Parliament and the country for imminent conflict. It fell to Dunglass to get a message to the Prime Minister while the latter was at the despatch box that Hitler had agreed to a third meeting with Chamberlain, this time at Munich, to try to save the peace. *I could not get directly at Chamberlain across the back of the Front Bench, so I handed the note to Sir John Simon. He took a second or two to absorb it and handed it on to the Prime Minister just before he sat down.*[14] Then, with the applause of the Commons still ringing in his ears and in such haste that he had to borrow a clean shirt from his brother's landlord, Dunglass accompanied his master to the infamous four-power conference. There, the Prime Minister shared with his young companion the feeling of personal contempt for Hitler which direct acquaintance had engendered, and the purpose behind the piece of paper which would soon be waved to adoring crowds in Downing Street. *If Hitler signed it and kept the bargain, well and good; alternatively … if he broke it, he would demonstrate to all the world that he was totally cynical and untrustworthy, and this would have its value in mobilising public opinion against him, particularly in America.*[15]

If Hitler signed it and kept the bargain, well and good; alternatively … if he broke it, he would demonstrate to all the world that he was totally cynical and untrustworthy.

DOUGLAS-HOME

When war finally came in September 1939 Dunglass still clung to the hope that an Italian initiative might yet lead to another negotiated settlement. It was not to be. From his personal point of view he made what was probably a tactical mistake in deciding to stay with Chamberlain rather than to enlist. In December he went with the Prime Minister to France – 'in uniform, but looking very unmilitary'[16] – to inspect the apparently formidable military arrangements in place on the front line, but he was slow to appreciate the steady erosion of Chamberlain's political position at home. Not until the eve of the crucial Norwegian debate in May 1940 did he realise the seriousness of the situation. Then, while remaining totally loyal to Chamberlain, he threw such weight as he had behind the idea of a Halifax premiership, should the incumbent fail to survive. Desperately, Dunglass tried to persuade the Prime Minister's Conservative critics to return to the fold in return for the dismissal of unpopular ministers. But it was too late. Chamberlain finally recognised that he was not the man to lead a united nation into the next and most threatening phase of the war and, with Halifax effectively ruling himself out of contention, it was Winston Churchill who now took his place. Dunglass met this development with scarcely concealed dismay. On the evening of Chamberlain's resignation he met with other loyalists and 'drank in champagne the health of the "King over the Water"'. It made one of them 'shudder' to think of Churchill's maverick associate, Brendan Bracken, sitting in the room previously occupied by the 'charming, inoffensive and extremely sensible Alec', but nothing could be done about it.[17]

> Brendan Bracken (1901–58) was a journalist and Conservative MP who was a staunch opponent of appeasement in the 1930s and a close ally of Winston Churchill during his so-called 'Wilderness Years'. After serving as Churchill's parliamentary private secretary, he replaced Duff Cooper as Minister of Information from 1941 to 1945, and was briefly First Lord of the Admiralty until the Conservatives were defeated in the 1945 general election. He was made a peer by Churchill in 1952, but died of cancer six years later. His Irish origins and maverick nature made him unpopular with more traditional Tories.

Dunglass saw that this was the time for him to enlist but, to his dismay, the Army Medical Board turned him down as unfit. After exhaustive examinations, it was revealed that he was suffering from tuberculosis of the spine, the result perhaps of a seemingly innocuous accident two years earlier.

The treatment involved taking flakes from his shinbone to graft on to the affected vertebrae. Dunglass was then encased in plaster with no guarantee that he would ever walk again. Not for Dunglass, then, any possibility of the sort of 'good war' which might have provided a launch-pad for his later political career. His time, however, was not wasted. Reading was the limit of his physical capacity and read he did, voraciously. For the first time, and with enormous implications for his role in post-war politics, his interest turned to the international scene. As he later explained, *I foresaw a deep political division within Europe following a long war; and if the Germans were defeated, an attempt by the Soviet Union to dominate the centre of the Continent. So I read all the books I could find on communism.*[18] From this intense period of enforced study there emerged the clear, strongly-held and sometimes over-simplified ideas that would characterise his later attitude and, in particular, his two periods as Foreign Secretary. The Soviet Union represented an abiding threat to the Western Democracies and the post-war situation would necessitate the closest co-operation with the United States.

By the summer of 1942 he was taking his first tentative steps. The treatment had been successful. His 'patience and courage throughout all this trying time have been wonderful' noted a fellow Tory MP.[19] Though Dunglass had not lost his earlier interest in social and economic issues – he was a founder member of the Progress Trust founded in 1945 – his political priorities had certainly changed. This was apparent when, with Germany in evident retreat, he began to make his mark again in the House of Commons in the autumn of 1944. The lesson of Munich, that it would never again be right to give in to a threatening aggressor, had been learnt, but Dunglass was clear that this lesson could not be selectively applied. Intervening in a debate in September he gave voice to the sort of fear which Churchill reserved for his more private moments of introspection. Was it right that the future of Poland should be settled on exclusively Soviet terms? *If, after the defeat of Germany, this gallant but unhappy people are still left in bondage, and if this country has failed to do anything that we ought to have done, or might have done, then our national conscience will be uneasy for generations.*[20] This intervention prompted one observer to link Dunglass with Quintin Hogg and Peter Thorneycroft, leading lights in the newly formed Tory Reform Committee, as 'the rising hopes of the moment'.[21]

Poland's future was a central issue when the Big Three, Churchill, Roosevelt and Stalin, met at Yalta in the Crimea in February 1945. With Soviet forces advancing rapidly into Central Europe, Dunglass appeared less appreciative of the weakness of Churchill's bargaining position than he had been of the predicament facing Neville Chamberlain in the late 1930s. When news came through of the agreements reached on Poland's frontiers, government and elections, Dunglass made a forceful intervention at the backbench 1922 Committee to protest at what he saw as a breach of the Atlantic Charter. He was disappointed at the lack of a commitment to include a substantial proportion of the London-based Polish government-in-exile in the country's new administration and the lack of international supervision for the promised elections. When Parliament debated the issue a fortnight later, he interrupted Churchill to seek clarification on this last point and then, in his own 'excellent' speech,[22] bitterly attacked the whole Polish settlement. With some prescience about the future pattern of Soviet diplomacy, he described Poland as the first test case in the relationship between *a great power wielding great military might and her smaller weaker neighbour.*[23] Dunglass was among 21 Conservative MPs who put down an amendment regretting that Polish territory had been trans-

ferred to another power. With Churchill's public pronouncements exuding confidence about the future course of relations
between the wartime allies, it was a brave step to take. But
Dunglass's evident sincerity commanded respect and there
was no lasting animosity on Churchill's part, Indeed when,
in May 1945, the Labour and Liberal parties withdrew from
the wartime coalition and Churchill formed his pre-election
caretaker government, Dunglass found himself entrusted,
on the recommendation of James Stuart, Conservative Chief
Whip and fellow Scot, with his first ministerial office, Under-
Secretary of State for Foreign Affairs.

The appointment might have been of significance if, as
expected, Churchill had emerged victorious from the subsequent general election. As it was, Dunglass scarcely had time
to put down a marker in the department in which he would
later make his most important political impact before he was
obliged to launch his campaign in Lanark. Few contemporary
observers understood the extent to which the political climate
had changed over the war years and, to the extent that they did
understand it, still could not believe that the electorate would
reward Churchill for his monumental contribution to victory
by dismissing him from office. Dunglass, however, soon had
reason to describe the campaign as the dirtiest in which he
had ever fought. Rumours abounded that his wartime illness
had been but a cover for clandestine activities and that his
stance in the 1930s reflected an innate sympathy for the
Nazis. Yet even without such complications it is doubtful if
he could have withstood the national tide in Labour's favour.
Lanark reverted to its more natural allegiance with Labour's
Tom Steele victorious by just under 2,000 votes.

The next five years were a relatively quiet period in Dunglass's life, and not unwelcome for that. They gave him the
opportunity fully to restore his health and to develop his

growing interest in foreign affairs without the daily distraction of the House of Commons and constituency business. It also afforded the possibility of spending more time with his growing family. Dunglass had married Elizabeth Alington, daughter of his old Eton headmaster, in October 1936. Three daughters were born over the next few years, followed by a son and heir, David, in November 1943. With the loss of his parliamentary seat, many assumed that Dunglass's political life was now effectively over. After all, his father was in his seventies and in relatively poor health. The Earldom of Home with its varied responsibilities, not to mention its likely barrier to further political advancement, could not lie too far in the future. But Dunglass was in fact re-adopted as prospective candidate for Lanark and quietly looked forward to recovering the seat from Labour. He took office as chairman of the Eastern Divisional Council of the Scottish Unionists and, in 1949, contributed to a party report entitled 'Scottish Control of Scottish Affairs' which recommended a greater measure of devolved powers. His public pronouncements, at a time of heightening Cold War tension, continued to focus on the Soviet menace. Friendship between nations, he told readers of *The Times*, could only grow on the basis of common moral and ethical principles and, while the Communists remained in charge of the Soviet Union, these principles could not exist.[24] But it was significant that he was not at the heart of Conservative politics at a critical time in the party's history when the shape of its post-war beliefs and policies was being moulded. Dunglass found himself isolated from a new generation of rising Tories who would one day dominate the upper echelons of the party. Labour's Prime Minister, Clement Attlee, called a general election for February 1950. Dunglass now showed that he was not as disdainful of the darker political arts as has sometimes been suggested. Shortly before the poll he arranged for a letter written by Steele in 1945 to be distributed at the MP's meetings. In it Steele had thanked members of the Communist Party for their help in his earlier campaign. Much had happened in world affairs over the intervening five years to change popular perceptions of the Far Left, but Dunglass's somewhat questionable tactics may have been critical in what proved to be a closely fought contest. By just 685 votes he regained his seat in the House of Commons.

Nationally, Labour just managed to cling on to power, though with a greatly reduced overall majority. Dunglass had to play his part in the systematic harrying of what was now a near-exhausted administration. With East-West tension steadily mounting, the theme of his speeches was entirely predictable. Western civilisation would be finished, he warned the Commons in November 1950, if Russia should get control of Germany and therefore of the continent of Europe.[25] But his return to the Commons was to be of short duration. On 11 July 1951 his father died and Dunglass immediately became the 14th Earl of Home. Despite poor health, the death itself was unexpected. Dunglass was dining in the Commons when he received the news. Even an innocent attempt to retrieve some papers from the chamber represented a technical infringement since the new peer was now a member of 'another place'.

'Go and quell those turbulent Scots and don't come back until you've done so.'

CHURCHILL TO DOUGLAS-HOME

If the defeat of 1945 had not drawn a line under his political career, this latest development seemed certain to have done so, and Home (as he will now be called) quickly reconciled himself to this fact. He remained a largely unknown figure outside Westminster and, in any case, it would not be long before a new and talented Tory intake, several years younger than himself and many of them associated with the so-called

'One Nation Group', began to make their mark. Not for the first or last time, however, fortune favoured him. When the ageing Churchill returned to Downing Street after the general election of October 1951, Home was offered and accepted the post of Minister of State for Scotland. *It seemed rather stodgy just to stay at home and live on your money and look after your estates*, he later explained.[26] Once again he owed his preferment to James Stuart who himself became Scottish Secretary. Home's appointment was a shrewd one, made at a time when Scottish nationalism was beginning to stir. His brief was to work mainly in Scotland, with only monthly appearances in the House of Lords, and to help dispel the growing feeling that the Scots were being taken for granted. He recalled Churchill's unembellished directive: 'Go and quell those turbulent Scots and don't come back until you've done so.'[27] Home worked well with Stuart who allowed him considerable autonomy. He proved adept at making speeches to small Scottish audiences, a task from which Stuart recoiled. Within weeks of his appointment he had announced the setting-up of a committee on the financial and economic relationship between Scotland and the United Kingdom as a whole. Its report proposed that Scottish revenue and expenditure accounts should in future be separately prepared. Home's responsibilities, which encompassed industry, including forestry and hill-farming, education and local government, give the lie to charges that were levied a dozen years later that he lacked experience on the home front. The difficulty then was more that his experience was out of date and had little relevance to the problems of an over-heating industrial economy. One of Home's more important legacies was the Crofters (Scotland) Act of 1955 which sought to reverse the decline in farming in the Highlands through the application of grants and loans to small-scale producers.

Churchill clung on to the premiership for longer than anyone, except perhaps himself, had anticipated back in 1951. Despite a near-fatal stroke in 1953 he remained Prime Minister until April 1955. Home retained his position at the Scottish Office throughout, despite the efforts of senior ministers such as Eden and Lord Salisbury to tempt him into their service. 'Your Home, Sweet Home seems to be doing well' was Churchill's assessment.[1] At a time when Scottish Toryism has become something of a minority interest, it is worth recalling that the Conservative party secured a majority of the popular vote north of the border at the general election of 1955. Perhaps then, it should not have been the occasion for any surprise that, seven weeks earlier, when Eden finally succeeded Churchill as Prime Minister, Home was singled out for promotion. Aged almost 52, he entered the Cabinet for the first time as Secretary of State for Commonwealth Relations. The appointment, which was coupled with the deputy leadership of the House of Lords, occasioned considerable comment, partly because it was one of the very few changes that Eden made to his predecessor's Cabinet and partly because, after his semi-exile in Scotland, Home remained an almost unknown figure as far as the general public was concerned.

The Commonwealth was a far more central concern in the calculations of the British government of the mid-1950s than it has since become. Memories of the largely spontaneous contribution of the self-governing Dominions to the British war effort were still gratefully recalled and almost every British family could count relatives or friends living in countries such as Australia and Canada. The Commonwealth was a key factor in Britain's continuing pretensions to world-power status and an important determinant of the approach of both the leading political parties towards the advancing process of European integration. This was very evident in the way in which Home took up the Commonwealth's cause when the Eden government considered its position in response to renewed integrationist stirrings on the continent. 'An excellent meeting of Economic Policy Ctee', noted the Euroenthusiast Harold Macmillan in September 1956. 'Only Home ... and David Lloyd (for Colonial Office) rather doubtful.'[2]

'Your Home, Sweet Home seems to be doing well.'

CHURCHILL

By the time that Home became its Secretary of State the future development of the Commonwealth had clearly taken a decisive turn. With the post-war Labour government's granting of independence to the Indian sub-continent in the late 1940s, the white exclusivity of the organisation was at an end. Even so, the mid-1950s was a relatively quiet time in the Commonwealth's history just before the high tide of African nationalism precipitated a further shift in the evolution of the old empire at the end of the decade. This relative leisure enabled Home to embark upon an extensive tour of Commonwealth countries in September 1955. A journey of 35,000 miles took him to Australia, New Zealand, Singapore, India, Pakistan and Ceylon and enabled him to meet significant figures on the world stage including Robert Menzies and Pandit Nehru. A speech delivered in Delhi in

October in which he warned that Britain had learnt the bitter lesson that weakness in the face of dictators only invited further aggression and that neutrality had no meaning in the context of totalitarian ambition did not go down well with the avowedly non-aligned Indian leader.

Before long, however, the Commonwealth came to the forefront of British politics, while the Secretary of State found himself closer to the heart of government than ever before. Home was a major player throughout the Suez Crisis of 1956. Present at the state banquet for King Feisal of Iraq on 26 July at which Eden learnt of Colonel Nasser's decision to nationalise the Suez Canal Company, he became a member of the Cabinet's Egypt Committee which directed British policy leading up to the invasion in the autumn, and he seems to have been a close confidant of the Prime Minister throughout the weeks of crisis. Above all, it fell to Home to prevent the disintegration of the Commonwealth itself as that organisation had to withstand the most divisive challenge in its history to date. Eden was no easy master to serve. The testimonies of Cabinet ministers of his inability to delegate, his compulsive tendency to interfere in the minutiae of their departmental business and his constant pestering and harassment are too numerous to ignore, and Home was by no means immune to this treatment. But Home seems to have been temperamentally better equipped to cope with Eden's excesses than were most of his colleagues. *I got on very well with him*, Home later declared. He was *such a nice chap and so good-mannered and charming that I did not mind*.[3] Correspondence between the two men at the height of the crisis suggests a mutual confidence and meeting of minds which the Prime Minister failed to achieve with some of his more senior colleagues.

Suez, of course, did lasting, perhaps irreparable, damage to Eden's reputation. In brief, the charge against him is that, thwarted of the chance of immediate military action to recover the canal, he resorted to a sordid, clandestine plot with Israel and France, by which the former was encouraged to invade Egypt and thereby provide Anglo-French forces with a pretext to reoccupy the canal zone to protect it from the consequences of military action, which had itself been wilfully engineered. To top it all, Eden then lied to the House of Commons in denying that this collusive negotiation had taken place. A variety of explanations have been put forward to explain the behaviour of a Prime Minister whose previous conduct throughout a long career in public life had been characterised by unimpeachable integrity. Did Eden's chronic ill-health fatally distort his judgement? Or had the demands of the premiership revealed the deficiencies of a man who, whatever his other qualities, was ill-equipped for the top job in British politics? Such factors may have been relevant, but the opening of government archives has confirmed that Eden did not act alone. Figures such as Home were fully privy to what was going on and their conduct and support for what Eden did cannot be explained by reference to the Prime Minister's health. Throughout the crisis, indeed, Home was among the Cabinet's hawks. Yet, somewhat ironically, his personal and political integrity have seldom been questioned.

Home's role over Suez (indeed, British policy as a whole) only really makes sense when placed in the broader context of great power relations that had become his abiding concern since the Second World War. Home was uneasy about Eden's plan and remained so for the rest of his life. *A case can be made*, he rather hesitatingly recalled. *I didn't like it. I didn't like it then; none of us liked it … it was a horrible situation to be in, the worst I've been in.*[4] Twenty years after the event his Cabinet colleague, Selwyn Lloyd, Eden's Foreign Secretary, decided to publish his account of what had happened. The charge of collusion, Lloyd recognised, would have to be faced. But 'collusion implies something dishonourable and we were all honourable men!'[5] British ministers were convinced, on the basis of probably faulty intelligence reports, which may be one of the most significant but least appreciated elements in the whole crisis, that Nasser should not be viewed in isolation but in the context of global Soviet strategy. *I was quite clear*, Home later insisted, *that Nasser's seizure of the Canal was part of a wider scheme in which the Russians were immensely inter-ested.*[6] His contemporary words are even more revealing: *I have no doubt that if we cannot make anything of the Security Council ... we have no option but to go through with it. I need not say more but I am convinced that we are finished if the Middle East goes and Russia and India and China rule from Africa to the Pacific.*[7] Such assessments may have been erroneous – Nasser was first and foremost an Arab nationalist rather than the tool of inexorable Soviet expansion – but they help make sense of what followed. Home and others were sure that it was no less than a question of Britain's survival as a great power. Such a challenge, they believed, justified extraordinary measures.

I was quite clear that Nasser's seizure of the Canal was part of a wider scheme in which the Russians were immensely interested.

DOUGLAS-HOME

As the crisis unfolded, it fell to Home to warn Eden of attendant pitfalls. Talks with the Canadian High Commissioner revealed that that Dominion at least could not be relied upon for support in the event that the use of force became unavoidable. He sensed a *definite wavering* in the attitude of some ministers towards military action.[8] Home noted doubts on the part of R A Butler, the Lord Privy Seal, and urged the Prime Minister to see him alone to offer reassurance. Part of the problem, he believed, was that Eden had 'pushed that vital decision [to use force] through Cabinet without time for a proper discussion'.[9] But he remained loyal to the Prime Minister throughout and connived in the blackout of information to which the Commonwealth was subjected prior to the Israeli attack on 29 October. While Eden entered the bear-pit of the Commons to defend the actions of the British and French governments, it fell to Home, in the absence of Lord Salisbury, to perform the same task in the somewhat less febrile atmosphere of the upper chamber. Here he emphasised in public his conviction that *our life* [was] *at stake* in the quest to thwart Nasser's adventures. Almost to the end, Home was determined to press on, regardless of the mounting chorus of world condemnation. To the beleaguered Premier he wrote with *unstinted admiration*: *If our country rediscovers its soul and inspiration your calm courage will have achieved this miracle.*[10] Not until 6 November, the day of the ceasefire, did Home's conviction waver. The sight of the American Sixth Fleet menacingly arrayed in the Mediterranean and the impact of United States' pressure on sterling finally persuaded him that the game was up. Though never shaking his belief that the Atlantic Alliance would remain fundamental to Britain's power and security, the actions of the Eisenhower administration left a lasting sense of grievance. *It was quite unnecessary for them to demonstrate their hostility with the Sixth Fleet movement. That was what stuck in my gullet.*[11]

Like others in the government Home could now do no more than put the best possible gloss on the situation. Britain had used her power to prevent the Middle East from bursting into flames. A general war had been stopped, and a communist plot foiled. The United Nations had been obliged to shoulder its responsibilities. In reality, of course, Britain had suffered a humiliating defeat. But Home's emollient manner was certainly important in soothing the ruffled feathers of several

Commonwealth countries and, in the event, none left the organisation. Suez ruined Eden's career. Even had ill-health not fortuitously intervened, it seems unlikely that he could have held on to the premiership. Home himself reached this conclusion before Christmas and 'rather grudgingly agreed' that Harold Macmillan would be the best choice to succeed.[12] It would be one of the latter's most polished achievements as Prime Minister to secure the government's recovery from the nadir of Suez without ever bringing himself to concede that the expedition had been ill-conceived. This meant allowing Eden, almost alone, to shoulder the burden of responsibility, while making as few changes to the government as possible. When, therefore, Macmillan formed his administration in January 1957, Home retained his position at the Commonwealth Office.

Set against the drama of Suez none of the rest of Home's concerns at the CRO was of comparable importance. But he did find himself dealing with a problem in southern Africa which would occupy much of his time in his remaining two decades on the front-line of British politics. Once British governments had recognised the need to divest themselves of their colonial empire, the path towards independent African states was assured. That

Harold Macmillan (1894–1986) had been on the anti-appeasement wing of the Conservative Party in the 1930s, and came into government when Churchill became Prime Minister in 1940. Closely involved in the Suez Crisis in 1956, he nonetheless succeeded Eden as Prime Minister and went on to win an unexpected election victory in 1959, and earned himself the nickname 'Supermac'. After his resignation in 1963 he went back to his family's publishing firm, though he accepted a peerage in 1984, criticising aspects of Margaret Thatcher's policies in the House of Lords. (See *Macmillan* by Francis Beckett, in this series.)

path would be impeded by many problems *en route* and the issue of timing would remain contentious, but the ultimate destination was now beyond dispute. But Southern Rhodesia was different. The existence of a sizeable white settler population of about a quarter of a million complicated any notion of an orderly transition to power for the black majority. Indeed, Southern Rhodesia had been granted a considerable measure of internal self-government as long ago as 1923. Then, 30 years later, in a move of questionable wisdom, Churchill's government had formed the Central African Federation in which Southern Rhodesia was coupled with Northern Rhodesia and Nyasaland. This had the effect of bolstering the position of the European minority and greatly complicating the process of Britain's ultimate withdrawal from colonial responsibility. The situation was further confused by a division of authority between government departments in London, for while Northern Rhodesia and Nyasaland fell under the jurisdiction of the Colonial Office, Southern Rhodesia and the Federation itself were the responsibility of the CRO. Such an arrangement would have been a recipe for dispute and friction had it not been for a broad meeting of minds between Home and the long-serving Colonial Secretary, Alan Lennox-Boyd.

Home's basic attitude towards the question of colonial development was realistic but out of step with the views of the political left and even with those of some of the more advanced members of his own party. He saw no particular virtue in the simple mantra of 'one man, one vote'. As he once put it, it had taken the British people 600 years to move from a qualified franchise to this position and, although it would be unrealistic to imagine Africans having to serve such a lengthy apprenticeship, a headlong rush to independence would create more problems than it would solve. In March 1960 he warned the House of Lords of the form of racialism which claimed Africa exclusively for the Africans. Increased African representation would need to be based on educational qualifications and this would take time. Political independence would require political maturity. Arguably, Home underestimated that growth of nationalist sentiment within the African continent to which Macmillan gave expression in his famous 'Wind of Change' speech to the South African parliament in February 1960. Certainly, his views were what a later generation would style 'politically incorrect', but the subsequent history of at least parts of independent Black Africa compels a reconsideration of Home's words: *The complete universal suffrage is only meaningful when the individual voter can exercise a free and unfettered choice between parties and when voters in the aggregate have learned not to misuse the vast majorities which often emerge from free elections.*[13]

Home struck up a good working relationship with Roy Welensky, the former heavyweight boxer, barman and engine driver who became Prime Minister of the Federation in 1956 and Welensky certainly saw in Home an ally in his determination to protect the interests of the settler population. Home largely accepted Welensky's contention that anything other than the most cautious British support for increased African participation could lead to the white population throwing its support behind overtly racist politics on the model of the apartheid regime in South Africa. But Home's problems multiplied after the 1959 general election when Lennox-Boyd retired and was replaced by Iain Macleod. Macleod was perhaps the one leading Conservative with whom Home, during his long political career, found it almost impossible to work. The new Colonial Secretary seemed determined to accelerate the pace of decolonisation much faster than Home considered wise. Unlike Home he had little time for the Central African Federation and before long there was an increasing tendency to identify the Colonial Office with the defence of African rights and to see the CRO as the guardian of European minorities.

Matters came to a head as a result of Macmillan's decision in 1959 to create a royal commission under Sir Walter Monckton to look into the Federation's continuing viability prior to a constitutional conference arranged for the following year. The Federal Government was immediately suspicious and it fell to Home to persuade Welensky, who took an instant dislike to Macleod, to accept the Commission in the first place. But he did so by dropping broad hints that the question of secession from the Federation by Northern Rhodesia and particularly Nyasaland would not be considered while a Conservative government remained in power in London. Following Macmillan's return from his African tour Macleod pressed for the release from prison of the Nyasaland nationalist leader, Hastings Banda, in order that he could give evidence to the Monckton Commission, a proposal bitterly opposed by the Welensky government. Home suggested flying out to Salisbury, the Southern Rhodesian capital, to seek a compromise. This he duly did, overriding complaints from the Cabinet Secretary that Banda's release was rightly a matter to be decided between the Governor of Nyasaland and the Colonial Secretary. In Salisbury Home found unrelenting opposition to Macleod's suggestion. Edgar Whitehead, the Southern Rhodesian Premier, could not have been more blunt. 'I tell you straight that if you release Banda in Nyasaland, Southern Rhodesia will blow up and leave the Federation and I shan't be able to stop them!'[14] Home's inclination was to give way and in London Macmillan was inclined to agree but, faced with the threat of Macleod's resignation, had to ask Home to try again. Finally, Home persuaded Welensky and Whitehead to agree to Banda's release on 1 April 1960.

This was three weeks later than Macleod had wished, but still allowed for a few days in which Banda, as a free man, could give his evidence to the Commissioners. 'Alec Home is a really splendid fellow,' recorded Macmillan with a considerable sense of relief. 'He fully understood the political dangers which would follow Colonial Secretary's resignation.'[15]

The future of the Federation remained unresolved at the time of Home's departure from the CRO. He personally was still thinking in terms of independence for Nyasaland and Northern Rhodesia no earlier than 1970. Macleod's preferred timetable was probably envisaged in terms of months. When Monckton reported in October, by which time Home had moved to the Foreign Office, it was clear that secession had indeed been on the agenda and that all three countries would eventually be given the right to go their separate ways. There is some evidence that Home was extremely annoyed by this outcome. But his transfer to another department avoided any serious ructions within the government. As it was, the Federation was dissolved in December 1963 and Northern Rhodesia and Nyasaland moved to independence as Zambia and Malawi respectively, leaving the issue of Southern Rhodesia, now renamed simply Rhodesia, no nearer a solution.

As a Cabinet minister Home started to become involved in matters of government policy beyond his departmental brief. This was particularly the case after he succeeded Lord Salisbury as Leader of the House of Lords following the latter's resignation in March 1957 when his position became 'one of special importance'.[16] As the government's leading spokesman in the upper chamber Home had to pronounce on a wide range of matters while giving notice, to at least a few perceptive observers, of his capacity for even wider responsibilities. Lord Kilmuir, the Lord Chancellor, later paid tribute to 'the extraordinary development of Lord Home in the House of Lords' as one of the key factors in the stabilisation of Macmillan's administration after the traumatic experience of Suez.[17] It was from his platform in the Lords that he warned of the continuing danger posed by the Soviet Union – *a potential enemy who will stop at nothing and for whom the end justifies the means* – and of the absolute necessity for Britain to retain its independent nuclear deterrent – *We cannot, and no Government could, transfer any important section of our defence to another country, however friendly.*[18] Some of his other views were protected by the confidentiality of Cabinet discussion. Home was one of the first ministers to argue for immigration controls. His words read somewhat uncomfortably half a century on. In a memorandum presented to the Cabinet in August 1955 he stressed that he did not wish to exclude immigrants of *good type* from the old Dominions, but was ready to discriminate against West Indians. More sympathetic to newcomers from the Indian sub-continent, he nonetheless believed that the rate of migration among working-class Indians *unless checked … could become a menace.*[19]

We cannot, and no Government could, transfer any important section of our defence to another country, however friendly.

DOUGLAS-HOME

He was a popular minister in his own department, showing an ability to deal with business briskly and efficiently and to reach decisions without undue delay. He was never overwhelmed by the paperwork which filled his red boxes. Home was also starting to advance inside the Conservative party. Under Macmillan a sort of inner cabinet emerged known as the Steering Committee, charged with focussing on policy for the next general election. Home joined it in 1958, taking his place alongside key strategists such as Macleod, Lord Hailsham and Edward Heath. Not all of his ideas, however, were well received. A by-election in Rochdale in February 1958 seemed to presage a worrying revival in the fortunes of the Liberal Party. Home favoured some form of Conservative-Liberal pact to assuage the disgruntled floating voter, but Macleod and Hailsham were implacably opposed. The Liberal tide soon turned. The idea was in any case probably a non-starter. The Liberal leader, Jo Grimond, was more interested in a realignment of the left than in an anti-socialist agreement with the Tories.

After five years as Commonwealth Secretary, Home was seen as one of the government's successes. Liked by his Cabinet colleagues and the party, if still comparatively unknown to the public at large, most importantly he enjoyed the support and respect of the Prime Minister. Home's were quintessentially a safe pair of hands. In all the circumstances his promotion to the Foreign Secretaryship in July 1960 should not have provoked quite as much surprise as it did. Macmillan was looking

John Selwyn Brook Lloyd, known as Selwyn Lloyd (1904–78) was first elected to Parliament in 1945, and was Foreign Secretary under Eden during the Suez Crisis, which he, like Macmillan, survived. Continuing as Foreign Secretary until appointed Chancellor of the Exchequer in 1960. Macmillan's sacking of him and six other cabinet ministers in 1962 in an attempt to refresh a weakened government became known as the 'Night of the Long Knives'. Having been Leader of the Commons under Douglas-Home, he became Speaker of the House of Commons from 1971 to 1976, when he went to the Lords.

to reshuffle his Cabinet because of the determination of the Chancellor, Derick Heathcoat Amory, to retire from frontline politics. Approached as to whether he would be prepared to replace Selwyn Lloyd at the Foreign Office if the latter moved to the Treasury, Home 'seemed rather flabbergasted but recovered slowly'.[20] Rumours of the appointment caused considerable outrage, with the press overwhelmingly hostile. Home was, insisted *The Times*, insufficiently distinguished. According to the *Mirror*, it would be 'MacWonder's Major Blunder', while the *Evening Standard* suggested that a group of influential Tory MPs were ready to tell the Prime Minister of their total opposition to Home's appointment. The *Sunday Express* objected to the choice of 'this unknown and faceless earl', while the *Daily Mail* advised Macmillan to stop making a fool of himself. Perhaps most tellingly, the *Mirror* condemned the 'ludicrous selection of the oh-so-dismal Lord Home' as the 'most reckless political appointment since the Roman Emperor Caligula made his favourite horse a consul', a characterisation previously bestowed upon the unfortunate Thomas Inskip, Baldwin's preferred choice over Churchill as Minister for the Co-ordination of Defence.

> '{The} most reckless political appointment since the Roman Emperor Caligula made his favourite horse a consul.'
>
> DAILY MIRROR

Writing in the *News of the World* Randolph Churchill dug up Home's past as a 'man of Munich' and expressed bewilderment that Macmillan could commit 'such an act of political indecency'. Characteristically, the new Foreign Secretary invited Churchill to lunch at the Ritz so that he could 'confirm his impressions and improve his copy'.[21] In the Commons the opposition leader, Hugh Gaitskell, also took up the Munich theme, though his argument that this threw into question Home's ability to negotiate successfully with the Soviet Union did scant justice to the consistent line the new Foreign Secretary had taken towards Russia over almost two decades. Gaitskell described the appointment as 'unnecessary and unwise' and as 'constitutionally objectionable' in that it involved going outside the House of Commons to fill one of the leading offices of state.[22] Foreign Secretaries in the Lords were by no means unknown. Chamberlain's appointment of Edward Halifax in 1938 had been the last example. But, two decades on, there was a widespread belief that such constitutional idiosyncrasies would not be repeated and it was known that Eden had drawn back from his selection of choice, Lord Salisbury, for precisely this reason. For Macmillan, however, nominating a peer had the positive advantage that it would make it easier for Home to carry out his international responsibilities across the world stage.

The clamour soon subsided. Conservative MPs rallied behind the Prime Minister, not least because Labour made the tactical error of tabling a motion of censure. Thus, after 57 years of comparative obscurity, Home now entered the full glare of media attention. How successful he would be in his new role was in large part dependent upon his relationship with Harold Macmillan. British Prime Ministers, especially those in their second and later terms of office, seem compelled to leave their mark on international affairs. Macmillan was no exception. Indeed, there has seldom been a premier as determined as he to keep the main lines of both economic and foreign policy in his own hands. Writing at the time of his own retirement three years later, Macmillan referred to the present policies of the Treasury and Foreign Office as ones which 'I initiated, approved and largely directed'.[23] Some indeed now saw Home as the sort of amiable figure of the second rank who would leave the Prime Minister's control largely undisturbed. The *Economist* suggested that he got on well with Macmillan by agreeing with him. There are elements of truth in this analysis. Macmillan's Cabinet dispositions were designed to ensure his own pre-eminence in setting the foreign policy agenda. But there is also a danger of underestimating the new Foreign Secretary's role and importance. Crucial to Home's partnership with Macmillan was the basic fact that the two men got on well together and liked and respected each other. They had much in common in terms of education and interests. Home was nearer to the Prime Minister in age and outlook than most of his Cabinet colleagues, especially after the wide-ranging reshuffle of July 1962. Above all, Home was from the sort of aristocratic background which Macmillan admired and valued, but to which he personally only aspired by marriage and association.

Both men had had enough experience of how the Prime Minister-Foreign Secretary relationship could become poisoned to strive to learn from past mistakes. To ensure that there would be no breakdown of relations between them, Home arranged that they should meet twice a week for 15 or 20 minutes for an off-the-record discussion without officials. This gave assurance that the two men would be singing from the same hymn-sheet and that the Foreign Secretary could rely on Prime Ministerial backing if a matter upon which they had already composed their thoughts came up before the Cabinet. It was the sort of relaxed but effective arrangement that would not have been possible during Eden's premiership. For the rest, Home was not unhappy for Macmillan to seek the diplomatic limelight; his own forté was for patient behind-the-scenes diplomacy. The only point of procedure upon which he seriously disagreed with the Prime Minister was as to the value of summit conferences. Home, his outlook overshadowed by Munich and Yalta, was doubtful whether intractable issues, which had defied conventional diplomatic practice, would suddenly yield to resolution at a high-profile heads of government meeting.

It was not the easiest of times for Home to enter the top echelons of the British government. Neither the domestic nor the international horizon looked particularly auspicious. On the home front it would not be long before the fortunes of the Conservative government began to wane. Macmillan himself rapidly lost that sureness of touch which had enabled him to restore his party's self-confidence after the low point of Suez and then to lead it to a crushing election victory in October 1959. Successive Chancellors of the Exchequer were unable to provide sustained growth without over-heating the economy. The new decade invited discussion of the country's relative decline and a series of publications appeared asking the uncomfortable question, 'What's wrong with Britain'. Intellectual opinion, badly shaken by Suez, was soon deserting the Conservatives and their political agenda. On the international front the Cold War was at its height. The Paris summit conference of May 1960 had collapsed in acrimony. Hopes of a relaxation of Soviet pressure in the post-Stalinist era had rapidly faded as world attention focused on a renewed crisis in Berlin. With hindsight historians would pinpoint 1960 as the year in which influential opinion began to abandon notions of Britain's world power role in favour of a more modest destiny inside the European Community.

Most incoming ministers need time to acquaint themselves with the problems facing their departments. But Home's basic ideas were already fixed. In particular, his views on how to deal with the Soviet Union had developed into a matter of firm conviction. *I had made up my mind*, he later recalled, *that the only way to deal with the leaders of the Soviet Union was to be strictly pragmatic*.[24] Their general objective remained to overturn capitalist and free societies, but they probably had no hard and fast blueprint as to how this would be achieved. Home professed no *innate hostility* to revolutionary Russia, *so long as the Communist leaders did not try to thrust the virtues of their dogma down other people's throats*.[25] Thus, rather as George Kennan had prescribed more than a decade earlier, the role of the West must be one of patient, long-term containment while never for one instant relaxing its guard. *Let up for one moment on vigilance, and everything which we value could be lost in the twinkling of an eye.*[26] It was as if Home more than anyone had learnt from the errors of the years of appeasement in the 1930s. *Reluctantly, but certainly, I came to one positive conclusion, that the Russian leaders would always take advantage of weakness, but – and here is a crumb of comfort – that they would not challenge equal or superior strength.*[27] This convinced him that it was the balance of nuclear terror which had maintained the peace of Europe since the end of the Second World War and which had forced the Soviets to back down at critical times. As a result, the maintenance of a European-North American, and specifically of an Anglo-American, axis through NATO had to be the linchpin of the British government's foreign policy. Aware that Britain's intrinsic power had declined sharply, he never wavered from the belief that the American alliance was of paramount importance. *I started with the premise that we had to engage America's sympathy and allegiance to a point where a President would take the supreme decision to drop the nuclear bomb to save Europe.*[28]

I started with the premise that we had to engage America's sympathy and allegiance to a point where a President would take the supreme decision to drop the nuclear bomb to save Europe.

DOUGLAS-HOME

The strength of Home's convictions made him a formidable negotiator. His tough stance over Berlin, where he was convinced that the Russians would eventually back down, helped dispel initial doubts about his suitability on the part of the West German Chancellor, Konrad Adenauer. Beneath his innate charm, his courtesy and his impeccable good manners, an American journalist sensed a 'certain tensile strength'.[29] Andrei Gromyko, the long-serving Soviet foreign minister, was more explicit. 'After talking to him for a while, one realised that something did not quite match his moderate manner. Resting now on one leg, now on the other, he would insist – quietly, of course – on expounding his ideas, without stopping, through to the bitter end.'[30] Some of his strongest words were reserved for the United Nations. That organisation's double standards were a matter of immense irritation to him, and he used an apparently innocuous address to the Berwick-on-Tweed United Nations Association in December 1961 to launch a stinging attack. While Third-World delegates missed no opportunity to put Britain into the international dock for the alleged crimes of colonialism, they tended to turn a blind eye to the tyranny and oppression existing behind the Iron Curtain. He feared that the Soviet Union was using the UN to prosecute the Cold War, *using racialism, nationalism and the exuberant individualism of newly independent countries to further their ends*.[31]

Andrei Gromyko (1909–89) was Soviet Foreign Minister for 28 years, from 1957 to 1985. Previously having been at the Soviet Embassy in the USA and at the UN, he was Ambassador to Britain 1952–3. The face of Soviet foreign relations throughout the Cold War, he was nicknamed 'Mr Nyet' or 'Grim Grom' for his obstinate negotiating style. He met with Kennedy during the Cuban Missile Crisis and helped negotiate all the arms limitation treaties of the period. He was ousted by Gorbachev in 1985 as an opponent of reform.

By the time that Home became Foreign Secretary, Macmillan's mind was already moving towards the desirability of British membership of the EEC. Edward Heath accepted appointment as Home's deputy and foreign affairs spokesman in the Commons only on the assurance that he would, as Lord Privy Seal, enjoy special responsibility for relations with Europe. But there was no fundamental conflict of interest. Home's own views were also moving in favour of British membership. He envisaged its advantages in terms of enhanced political clout in the wider world, but was anxious that special terms should be negotiated to accommodate the interests of the Commonwealth. Furthermore, he never saw the issue as a choice between Europe and the United States. Britain should be intimately connected with both. If he appreciated that Britain's great power days lay in the past, he was still determined that the country should, to the fullest extent possible, remain a major player on the world stage. More than four decades on, critics might suggest that his assessment of the situation lacked insight and understanding. He was apt to dismiss those who warned of the dangers of European federalism. *I doubt if the issue will ever be joined*, he told one journalist. *Here and there we may have to surrender a little sovereignty. But the basic issue is unlikely to come up.*[32] As negotiations progressed, the government played down the whole question of sovereignty, with Home telling the Lords that its surrender was restricted to economic matters – for all the contrary evidence within the Treaty of Rome. But neither Home nor any other minister could do anything to counter the determined and highly individualistic opposition

Sir Edward Heath (1916–2005) was appointed Conservative Chief Whip in 1955, and his report on backbench opinion on the succession to Eden after Suez helped Macmillan to win the leadership. In 1965 he was the first Conservative leader to be elected by the parliamentary party, and the youngest in its history, winning the 1970 election against all predictions. A fervent pro-European, he negotiated Britain's entry into the EEC, but was defeated by Wilson in 1974. Ousted by Margaret Thatcher in 1975, he remained in the Commons and saw her own downfall in 1990.

of the French President, General de Gaulle, who delivered an emphatic 'non' to the British application in January 1963.

Home's previous ministerial responsibilities ensured that he would, as Foreign Secretary, continue to take a lively interest in the affairs of the African continent. His last weeks as Commonwealth Secretary had been overshadowed by the possibility of South Africa's withdrawal from the Commonwealth, and the question remained unresolved when he assumed his new post. When the step was finally taken in May 1961 his feelings were divided. He recognised that apartheid was wrong, but never regarded it with the passion of those who felt it was so wicked as to place the country which practised it beyond the diplomatic pale. Home remained convinced that South Africa had an important role to play in building economic prosperity and in contributing to the security not only of the African continent but of the whole western world. Elsewhere on the continent there were renewed clashes with Iain Macleod. The latter's idea of releasing the Kenyan nationalist leader, Jomo Kenyatta, was, the Foreign Secretary insisted, *repugnant to decent-minded people*.[33] Macmillan's diary reveals that Home came near to resignation over the question of Northern Rhodesia in June 1961. He continued to resist the Colonial Secretary's drive to rapid Africanisation. *Anyone*, he conceded, *can give a country independence without worrying about the result but if the aim is to launch a nation … which is capable of surviving economically and will conduct its foreign relations according to the code of the good neighbour, it all becomes much more complicated*.[34] Macleod's departure to become Leader of the Commons in October came as a considerable relief to the Foreign Secretary.

Britain, however, was not the only country struggling to extricate itself from its imperial past. The legacy of Belgian rule in the Congo burst on to the international agenda during

1960 when the province of Katanga declared its separation from the newly independent state. Home was reluctant to support UN action to maintain the unity of the Congolese state and thus tended to give the Katangan leader, Tshombe, encouragement in his separatist adventure. At the back of the Foreign Secretary's mind was the fear of setting a precedent which might encourage UN interference in the still unresolved problems of Rhodesia. The episode involved some conflict with the Americans since President Kennedy was fully behind UN involvement. If such evidence were needed, the Congo demonstrated that Britain was now unlikely to prevail against the will of the United States. Katanga's secession formally ended in January 1963.

Home drew greater satisfaction from his efforts in relation to the South-East Asian state of Laos. The Americans tended to view that country in terms of their simplistic theory of falling dominoes. Laos had to be held or else the whole of the region would fall under communist domination. But patient and persuasive British pressure on Kennedy and Averell Harriman led to a softening of the American line and a ceasefire was arranged between the Laotian government and the communist insurgents in July 1962. For Home it showed the value of close partnership with the United States and he subsequently pressed for increased British investment in Laos to please the American government.

It was a feature of international affairs at this time that the trouble spots of the Cold War, once a largely European phenomenon, could erupt in all parts of the globe. Indeed, it was during Home's tenure of the Foreign Office that one such eruption brought the world closer than ever before or since to nuclear armageddon. The Cuban Missile Crisis of October 1962 starkly revealed the reality of Britain's status in world affairs. The supreme questions of war and peace rested in the hands of the leaders in Washington and Moscow. Macmillan, as the head of America's leading ally, played a significant role as a sounding-board for Kennedy's thoughts and a source of reassurance to him, but it is hard to discern genuine British influence at the policy-making level. Home was closer to Macmillan during these anxious days than any other Cabinet minister. He was, for example, present during the lengthy hot-line telephone conversations that crossed the Atlantic between President and Prime Minister – comforter and support to Macmillan as the latter was in turn to the President. But that was the effective limit of his power to shape events. Home knew that an American blockade of Cuba was of doubtful legality, but he had no wish to rock the boat of Anglo-American solidarity at such a time, by expressing such doubts. He remained remarkably calm throughout the 13-day crisis, telling the Cabinet that he did not believe that the Soviet leader, Khrushchev, wanted to start a war. *It was more probable that he was seeking to improve his bargaining position, particularly in relation to Berlin, and that he wanted the US government to appreciate from their own experience the Soviet reaction to the presence of US missile bases in Europe close to Russia and their determination to secure their removal.*[35] Only if the Americans lost their nerve was there a real danger of nuclear war. In the light of subsequent revelations this seems a remarkably accurate analysis on the Foreign Secretary's part. Out of the crisis there emerged, somewhat paradoxically, a genuine lessening of tension of which the clearest manifestation was the conclusion of a Partial Test Ban Treaty in Moscow in August 1963. For Britain it was a seminal moment, effectively the last occasion on which she would occupy a seat at

'The one star that has continued to climb to a meridian of respect and influence has been that of a peer – Lord Home.'

THE TIMES

the top table of international diplomacy. Home could take some credit for this achievement, a welcome boost to Macmillan's now increasingly troubled government. Yet there was significance in the Prime Minister's selection of Lord Hailsham to head the British delegation to Moscow.

As Foreign Secretary Home had confounded his domestic critics. Within a year of his appointment *The Times* was forced to concede that 'the one star that has continued to climb to a meridian of respect and influence has been that of a peer – Lord Home'.[36] Something of a pattern was emerging. As at the Scottish Office and as Commonwealth Secretary, he had performed better than expected and had grown with the job. His integrity and straightforwardness impressed. Those who worked with and for him liked his down-to-earth manner and his capacity to present a case lucidly and without unnecessary complications. Conservatives approved of his readiness to do unpopular things. His visit to Franco's Spain in 1961 excited the wrath of Labour's Michael Foot, but probably enhanced the Foreign Secretary's wider standing. A few perceptive observers began to consider the apparently impossible – that Home might rise yet further up the greasy political pole. Writing in the *New Statesman* in December 1962 Anthony Howard speculated that, in the event of Macmillan stepping down before the next general election, the succession would lie between Home and R A Butler with the former, especially if he enjoyed the Prime Minister's backing, likely to prevail. What Howard would not have known, however, was that a month earlier Macmillan had told Butler that Home was the only minister who could replace him – a remark which, at this stage, probably said more about his attitude towards the nominal deputy premier than it did about his assessment of the Foreign Secretary. Problems, of course, remained. The last peer to be Prime Minister had been the 3rd Marquess of Salisbury at the very beginning of the century. But in 1963 Anthony Wedgwood-Benn's long battle to disclaim his father's peerage finally forced a change in the law. Richard Crossman now noted 'the possibility of the Lords Hailsham and Home taking their chance, because they will soon be free to become members of the Commons'.[37] Whether Home would wish to follow such a course was, however, an entirely different matter. *I had a constituency once*, he told a Foreign Press Association lunch in July 1962. *I know what it is like, and I am not terribly anxious to have another*.[38] For all that, the prospect of the 14th Earl of Home becoming Prime Minister of Great Britain could no longer be ignored.

Chapter 3: The Succession (1963)

The process by which Alec Home became Prime Minister and leader of the Conservative Party remains the most controversial episode of his long political career. Much documentary evidence has now become available, but uncertainty persists, not least because a precise interpretation of what happened lies hidden in the inner thoughts and intentions of the key participants – Macmillan and Home himself – and of some members of the supporting cast, including the Lord Chancellor, Viscount Dilhorne, and the Chief Whip, Martin Redmayne. What now seems certain is that Home was a more active participant in events than was once thought. 'Considering how many hearts have been broken in pursuit of the glittering prize', wrote the seasoned journalist James Margach, Home was unique. 'He never lifted a finger to grab the Premiership.'[1] But it would be 'foolish to present Home as a political virgin unaware of his opportunity, for unambitious men do not devote 40 years to politics, however strong their sense of duty'.[2]

What is clear is that by the summer of 1963, the Partial Test Ban Treaty notwithstanding, the fortunes of the Conservative government were at a low ebb. Little had gone right for the Prime Minister over the previous two years. Problems with the management of the economy, together with a feeling that the government needed to be revitalised, had prompted him to sack one third of his Cabinet, including the Chancellor, Selwyn Lloyd, in the celebrated reshuffle of July 1962, a move that was widely interpreted as a sign of panic on the part of the once 'unflappable' Macmillan. Meanwhile the government became mired in a succession of security and sex scandals, culminating in the Profumo Affair when the Secretary of State for War was obliged to resign after lying to the House of Commons over his liaison with a society call-girl who was also sharing her favours with a naval attaché from the Russian embassy. What a later generation called 'sleaze' threatened to drag down Macmillan's administration just as assuredly as it did John Major's three decades later. At the policy level the Conservatives seemed, after 12 years in office, to have run out of steam. De Gaulle's veto on Britain's application for membership of the Common Market was a particular blow which left the Prime Minister seemingly uncertain which way to turn. And to cap it all, Harold Wilson, leader of the Labour Party since Gaitskell's sudden death in January 1963, was emerging as one of the most accomplished political operators of the post-war era, able to tap into the mounting public mood for change to transform British society and turn it over, refreshed and re-invigorated, into the hands of a younger generation. Strange as the comparison may now seem, Wilson was having some success in presenting himself as a British version of John F Kennedy, the youthful President of the United States. In this climate Macmillan appeared increasingly anachronistic, the survivor of an earlier generation out of touch with the modern world and with the society over which he nominally presided.

Conservative minds turned inevitably to the next general election, which would need to be held by the autumn of 1964 at the latest, by which time Macmillan himself would be 70 years of age. Even before ill-health forced his hand in the autumn of 1963, the question of the succession was a matter of open debate. On the issue of whether he should himself lead the party into the next election Macmillan's own mind wavered. By this stage Home had become one of his closest political confidants and the two men appear to have discussed the question together on several occasions. In September the Prime Minister recorded that Home was 'very distressed' to think that Macmillan had any idea of retiring, but that he could understand why such a course might be desirable.[3] Their consensus seems to have been that Macmillan should soldier on until early 1964, thus leaving his successor time to prepare himself and the party for an election later that year. Who that successor should be was, however, a matter of considerable uncertainty. The obvious candidate was R A Butler, a senior minister since the formation of the Conservative government in 1951, Macmillan's nominal deputy and a leading architect of the transformation of the post-war Tory party. Yet it is hard to escape the conclusion that Macmillan was determined to avoid having Butler succeed him. Since becoming Prime Minister he had kept Butler out of the two posts – Chancellor and Foreign

Harold Wilson (1916–95) had worked in the Ministries of Supply and Labour during the Second World War, and entered Parliament in 1945 in the Labour landslide election victory. Attlee made him President of the Board of Trade in 1947, and he was Shadow Chancellor under Gaitskell, succeeding him as Labour leader in 1963. This background of economic expertise, middle-class meritocracy and relative youth was placed in sharp contrast with the image Macmillan and Douglas-Home projected. He was Prime Minister 1964–70 and 1974–6, and the most electorally successful Labour leader until Tony Blair. (See *Wilson* by Paul Routledge, in this series.)

Secretary – which might have provided him with an irresistible momentum towards the succession. Furthermore, there was strong opposition to Butler inside the parliamentary party, particularly among its right wing, and the chairman of the 1922 Committee, John Morrison, had already let him know that 'the chaps won't have you' and that there was a strong desire for a leader of a younger generation.[4] This stipulation, whatever else it implied, appeared to exclude Home who was just seven months Butler's junior and to point, for the time being at least, to Reginald Maudling, the 46-year-old Chancellor of the Exchequer.

Macmillan's own preference was moving, if without total conviction, in the direction of Lord Hailsham. Relations between the two men had not always been easy and Hailsham had not been rewarded with the high office he might have expected after his contribution as Party Chairman to the 1959 election victory. But Macmillan had come to the conclusion that the combination of Hailsham's intellect, passion and charisma offered the party its best hope of a fourth successive victory at the polls. Hailsham's appearance alongside Averell Harriman and Andrei Gromyko in the final stages of the negotiations leading to the Partial Test Ban Treaty seemed to indicate that Macmillan envisaged a higher role for him in the near future. Strikingly too, when Home and Macmillan discussed the question on 18 September, the Foreign Secretary also came down in favour of Hailsham, while expressing the fear that there would be 'complete disunity in the Party, and that great troubles will follow'.[5]

Hailsham's eligibility for the leadership – and Home's too for that matter – resulted from a government bill to allow hereditary peers to renounce their titles. The original bill offered the right of immediate disclaimer only to newly inheriting peers; their existing lordships would have to await the dissolution of Parliament – in practice, the next general election – for the same right. But a Lords' amendment in July 1963, accepted by the government, removed this restriction, thereby opening up the race for the Conservative succession to reluctant members of the upper house. Unlike Hailsham, Home was not believed to be in this category. Indeed, there is evidence that Home might have been Macmillan's first choice to succeed him had the Prime Minister thought that the 14th Earl could be persuaded to renounce his inheritance – a somewhat curious selection if Macmillan really was attracted by Hailsham's particular combination of qualities, none of which was obviously present in Home. But others were less inclined to accept Home's reluctance to return to the Commons as his final word. Visiting John Morrison in the unusual surroundings of the latter's holiday home on the island of Islay in July, Edward Heath was told that Home should be encouraged to throw his hat, or his coronet, into the ring. Then, on the very day that the Lords Reform Bill reached the statute book, Morrison informed Home himself that the needs of the party might require him to be drafted. The Foreign Secretary's response was non-committal, but at least did not firmly rule out the possibility. This approach suggested that it was less Butler's age than his politics which made the deputy premier an unacceptable option. Meanwhile Hailsham and Home had discussed the matter together and reached an informal agreement that, whatever happened, it would not be possible from the point of view of the government's position in the House of Lords for them both to renounce their titles.

By early October, however, Macmillan, convincing himself of a 'growing wave of emotion' in his favour, resolved to fight another general election as leader.[6] At a meeting of the Cabinet on 8 October, from which the Prime Minister had discreetly withdrawn, ministers agreed to accept this decision but also considered the situation that would arise if ill-health prevented Macmillan from carrying out his intention. The Lord Chancellor, Lord Dilhorne, declared that, as he would in no circumstances be a candidate for the succession, he would be available to help with the necessary consultations in such an eventuality. Home, somewhat unnecessarily, added that he was in the same position and would be prepared to assist Dilhorne in this task. In all probability this represented the Foreign Secretary's honest assessment of the situation at that time, but he never believed that he had made anything in the nature of a solemn pledge from which he could not honourably be released. Others, however, would see the matter differently. When, therefore, at the end of this meeting, members of the Cabinet left for Blackpool where the annual party conference was about to begin, they could reasonably assume that, if Macmillan's health did fail, Home would not be a contender and that both he and Dilhorne had put themselves into the position of honest brokers between whoever chose to contest the succession.

> **Quintin Hogg** (1907–2001) entered Parliament in 1938 as a supporter of Chamberlain's Munich agreement, but his Commons career ended when he inherited the title of Lord Hailsham. He held a number of government posts in the Lords and was Conservative Party chairman 1957–9. Having renounced his peerage in 1963 to run for the leadership, in 1970 Heath appointed him Lord Chancellor, restoring him to the peerage. Serving until 1974, and then again from 1979 to 1987 under Margaret Thatcher, he was the longest-serving Lord Chancellor of the 20th century (11 years, 9 months).

At this point fate intervened. Macmillan had been obviously unwell before withdrawing from the Cabinet meeting. Within hours he had convinced himself that his condition was life-threatening and had decided to stand down. As the Prime Minister entered hospital, Butler travelled to Blackpool on 9 October and took up residence in Macmillan's suite at the Imperial Hotel, a symbolic gesture whose significance was unlikely to be missed. Home, still in London, visited Macmillan at the King Edward VII Hospital for Officers and was entrusted, in his capacity as that year's President of the National Union of Conservative Associations, with a statement to be delivered to the conference announcing the Prime Minister's resignation. Macmillan urged Home to consider his own credentials for the succession, but at the same time encouraged his son Maurice and his son-in-law Julian Amery to support Hailsham's candidature in Blackpool. Butler came to attach particular significance to the Foreign Secretary's hospital visit, believing that Home had in effect extracted the statement from the Prime Minister for his own advantage. Certainly, Maurice Macmillan believed that his father had had no intention, before Home's intervention, of making a public announcement of his resignation at this stage. When Home arrived at the Conference and read out Macmillan's letter, it was the first that the majority even of the Cabinet had heard of the Prime Minister's change of plan. At a stroke the normally staid annual assembly was transformed into something of a cross between a political beauty contest and an American presidential convention, an atmosphere that was felt likely to favour Hailsham whose stock was highest among the Conservative grass roots. At the end of a rambling speech to a fringe meeting later that evening, Hailsham emotionally

'A comparatively new name is beginning to be "talked up" in the Conference and hotel lobbies: the Earl of Home, Foreign Secretary.'

THE DAILY TELEGRAPH

announced his intention to renounce his peerage. In the short term, and rather like David Cameron 42 years later, he took the conference by storm. But there the parallel ended. The Hailsham bandwagon stalled almost before it got moving. Senior figures found his performance, including bringing his young baby to the conference, distasteful, confirming doubts that, however powerful his intellect, Hailsham's judgement could not be trusted. The arrival from America of Randolph Churchill, ready to dispense 'Q' for Quintin badges to all and sundry, did little to help Hailsham's cause.

By the time that the conference drew to a close, therefore, no clear front-runner had emerged. Neither Butler nor Maudling did much for their chances by their lacklustre speeches to the party faithful. But it was noted that Home's scarcely sparkling address on foreign affairs prompted an enthusiastic standing ovation. The political correspondent of the *Daily Telegraph* had already reported that 'a comparatively new name is beginning to be "talked up" in the Conference and hotel lobbies: the Earl of Home, Foreign Secretary'.[7] By the end of the week Home had received a steady stream of visitors urging him to come forward as a compromise candidate since a Hailsham-Butler contest was likely to produce deadlock. These included Dilhorne, Duncan Sandys and John Hare among Cabinet ministers and such influential backbenchers as Selwyn Lloyd, William Anstruther-Gray and Charles Mott-Radcliffe. Dilhorne's presence among this group suggested that he was already making the transition from honest broker to committed partisan, while Lloyd's involvement was particularly significant given his recent travels around the constituencies which were believed to have given him an insight into the views of party activists. Support for Home was also evident at a meeting of the 1922 Committee Executive, just before Butler's closing speech to the conference. Here it was agreed that Home was the only candidate capable of promoting the unity which the party desperately needed. Lunching with Home on 12 October, Butler was taken by surprise to learn that the Foreign Secretary intended to consult his doctor, a clear indication that he was preparing to enter the contest. But many senior figures remained opposed. Hailsham sought to convince Home that he lacked the necessary experience on the home front. 'He reminded me that he had been Minister of State in the Scottish Office. "That", I replied, "is not enough. They would skittle you out in six months."'[8] In like vein, Macleod and Maudling, sharing a railway carriage on the return journey from Blackpool, agreed that Home's leadership would make a mockery of everything they had tried to achieve since the war in terms of broadening the Conservative Party's popular appeal.

Back in London the key development was Macmillan's rapid change of horses from Hailsham to Home as the man most likely to stop Butler. 'They have all returned to London with the dilemma unresolved', noted the Prime Minister's Press Secretary. 'In opting for Hailsham the PM was proceeding on the assumption that Home was not in the field. He has now to swap horses.'[9] Macmillan met Dilhorne and the Chief Whip, Martin Redmayne, on Monday, 14 October. Though in principle 'Hoggites', they had been upset by Hailsham's undignified behaviour in Blackpool. 'It was thought that he need not have paraded the baby and the baby food in the hotel quite so blatantly or talked so much at large.'[10] If this intervention was not enough to scupper Hailsham's chances, the Foreign Secretary's meeting with Macmillan the following day provided the *coup de grâce*. Once again, the evidence suggests that Home played a much less passive role than was once believed. According to Home, David Ormsby-Gore, the British ambassador in Washington, had reported that a Hailsham premiership would deal a tremendous blow to Anglo-American relations 'and would in fact end the special relationship'. Furthermore, 'the incidents at Blackpool had alarmed Lord Home. He had thought that they might be the result of the man being a show-off. He now believed that it was because the person concerned was actually mad at the time.' Hailsham was frequently emotional and not always able to control his temper in public. But the charge of madness was surprising, especially coming from one not known for his use of over-extravagant language. To complete his case, however, Home claimed that Hailsham was thought to be right-wing and would therefore lose the party some votes on the left, a curious assessment granted the respective views of the two peers.[11] Following his meeting with Macmillan, Home confirmed to Selwyn Lloyd that, if majority opinion was found to favour him, he would accept the Queen's commission if sent for to form a government. The difficulty of both he and Hailsham leaving the Lords at the same time could, he now believed, be overcome by persuading Alan Lennox-Boyd to assume new responsibilities in the upper house.

The mechanism now employed to sound out party opinion – the so-called 'customary processes' from which Home emerged as Prime Minister – has been the subject of considerable commentary. Much of it has, however, overlooked the fact that no 'customary processes' actually existed in the sense of an agreed *modus operandi* and the procedure followed on this occasion differed considerably from that employed by the party at the time of Eden's resignation in January 1957. Macmillan set out a new procedure in a letter to Butler on 14 October and this was subsequently accepted by the Cabinet. Dilhorne would assess the opinions of the Cabinet; Redmayne those of Conservative backbenchers and junior ministers. Lord St Aldwyn would carry out a similar task among Tory peers. Finally, Lords Poole and Chelmer would seek opinion from the grass roots. A number of points should be noted. First, Macmillan managed to give the impression that, even if the soundings themselves were quickly completed, no precipitate action would be taken determining the succession. 'These consultations may take a day or two. I would like to be informed when they have been completed and I will at that time decide according to the state of my health what steps should then be taken.'[12] Second, all of those charged with gathering the necessary information were, with the exception of Poole, already among Home's declared adherents. Third, it was clear that this was not to be a simple counting of heads, and that Macmillan would be left to interpret the data before passing on a recommendation to the Queen.

Most controversy surrounds the role of Lord Dilhorne. He had begun the process of sounding out views at Blackpool. John Boyd-Carpenter felt there had been 'a touch of incongruous farce about sitting on the Lord Chancellor's unmade bed, while he, his massive frame poised in a creaking wooden chair, made a note of the view of a Cabinet Minister as to who should be Prime Minister of England'.[13] Dilhorne duly reported that ten ministers favoured

Richard Austen ('Rab') Butler was born in India in 1902. An MP from 1929, he was President of the Board of Education under Churchill during the war and Chancellor of the Exchequer from 1951 to 1955, during which time he deputised for Churchill during his illnesses. Widely thought to be a future Prime Minister, each time he lost out, first to Eden, then Macmillan (he was Home Secretary 1957–62) and finally Douglas-Home. After serving as Foreign Secretary in Douglas-Home's short-lived government, he retired from the Commons in 1965, going to the Lords as Baron Butler of Saffron Walden. He died in 1982.

Home, four Maudling, three Butler and two Hailsham. His figures seem inherently improbable, given the known preferences of several of those polled. Iain Macleod was listed among the Foreign Secretary's adherents, a strange inclusion granted his refusal to serve under him a few days later. And even if some Machiavellian explanation may be adduced for Macleod's vote, it is difficult to extend this to Sir Edward Boyle, also noted by the Lord Chancellor as a Home man. A charitable interpretation might be that Dilhorne reached the questionable conclusion of preponderant positive support for Home on the basis of an absence of outright hostility towards him on the part of most members of Macmillan's Cabinet. If true, this was a curious adjustment of the facts by an experienced lawyer. Rumours persisted, particularly after the publication of Macleod's version of events the following January, that Dilhorne had deliberately massaged the figures to reach the conclusion that both he and Macmillan by now desired.

Redmayne's figures on the preferences of the parliamentary party are naturally more difficult to verify. What is striking, however, is that he took up the suggestion from St Aldwyn that Home's name should be mentioned to MPs as the candidate most likely to unite the party. The Chief Whip told the Prime Minister that Home had a narrow lead among MPs polled, together with most second preferences and the lowest number of declared opponents. But it was not just the quantity of Home's support which impressed Redmayne, but also its quality. 'Maudling's is almost exclusively from the younger and more junior element. That given to Home and Butler is more mature but Home's covers a far wider cross-section of the Party.' The Chief Whip could not 'fail to come to the opinion that [Home] would be best able to secure united support'.[14] Reginald Bevins, the Postmaster-General and one of the few men of working-class origins to prosper in

Macmillan's government, was no doubt among those whose opinion the Chief Whip dismissed '"What about the peers – Alec and the other one,"' he recalled Redmayne asking. 'I said "Not at any bloody price."'[15] More typical perhaps was the experience of the young James Prior. After stating his preference for Maudling with Butler as second choice, he was induced to concede that Home could be a possibility. 'I have little doubt that even at that early stage I was put down as an Alec supporter.'[16]

With the House of Lords and the wider party also reporting substantial backing for the Foreign Secretary, all the pieces required for Home's succession were now falling into place. Indeed, when on 16 October Freddy Erroll, the President of the Board of Trade, suggested to Redmayne that the succession should go to Maudling, he was told that it was already too late. 'It's all arranged – it's going to Alec Home.'[17] Macmillan now prepared a memorandum of advice for the Queen which he duly read out to her when she visited him in hospital two days later. As Hailsham later put it, 'never before in the history of the office of Prime Minister had advice as to his possible successor been tendered from a bed of sickness, based on hearsay evidence prepared for him by others which he apparently had no possible means of verifying'.[18] Macmillan, who had now tendered his own resignation, couched his advice in the sort of terms which certainly appealed to himself and in all probability to the Queen as well. The latter readily agreed that Home was the most likely candidate to secure general support as well as being the strongest character. In Home the Queen had the prospect of welcoming a Prime Minister with interests and background far closer to her own than was the case with any of the alterna-

'It's all arranged – it's going to Alec Home.'

MARTIN REDMAYNE

tive contenders. But in accepting Macmillan's analysis she, at least in the opinion of her biographer, engaged in 'the biggest political misjudgement of her reign'.[19]

Speed, however, was now of the essence. As Macmillan was fully aware, the Cabinet's anti-Home forces had belatedly appreciated how rapidly events were moving and had spent the previous evening burying their differences and rallying behind Butler's candidature. A midnight meeting at the home of Enoch Powell, supplemented by a series of anxious telephone calls, resulted in a ministerial alliance fully capable of blocking Home's succession. As Powell recalled, seven Cabinet ministers 'declared, to Mr Butler and to one another, that they did not consider Lord Home should be Prime Minister, that they would serve under Mr Butler, and that they would not serve under Lord Home unless Mr Butler had previously agreed to do so'.[20] The seven dissidents were Macleod, Maudling, Hailsham, Boyd-Carpenter, Erroll, Boyle and Powell. This alliance does not throw such a searching question-mark over Dilhorne's figures as might first appear. These were men who now declared in favour of Butler as a means of stopping Home; not all had been Butler adherents as first choice. But it does show that Dilhorne's assessment that Home was the figure best able to unite the Cabinet was way off the mark. Indeed, using the Redmayne principle that one vote was not necessarily equal to any other and applying it now to the Cabinet, it is clear that such a combination of senior ministers, containing as it did all the other serious contenders for the succession, should have been powerful enough to stop the Home bandwagon in its tracks. The latter would not have been able to form a credible government if Butler, Hailsham, Maudling and Macleod had all held aloof. Redmayne himself was called to the midnight meeting and announced that plans were already afoot for Home to return to the Commons via an impending by-election in Scotland – a disclosure which came as a particular surprise to Macleod who, as Leader of the Commons, could reasonably have expected to be consulted about such a proposal.

In this situation Macmillan urged the Queen to act as quickly as possible. 'I said that I thought speed was important and hoped she would send for Lord Home immediately – as soon as she got back to the Palace. He could then begin to work. She agreed.'[21] Within hours, therefore, Home himself was at Buckingham Palace, not yet to kiss hands as Her Majesty's First Minister, but charged to see whether he could command sufficient support to form an administration. This development proved crucial. To stop Home before he had received this royal commission was one matter; to do so afterwards quite another. As the Queen's biographer has put it, 'it was soon clear that the Queen, bounced by Macmillan into asking Home, had effectively bounced most of the Cabinet into accepting him'.[22]

Reginald Maudling (1917–79) had been made Chancellor of the Exchequer by Macmillan following the 'Night of the Long Knives', and was popular in the party and the country when the leadership issue arose, but was thought to be too junior and did not perform well at the party conference. He was defeated for the leadership by Heath in 1965, and served as his Home Secretary from 1970–2. He was Shadow Foreign Secretary under Thatcher but was sacked in 1976 for opposing her economic and foreign policies. He died in 1979.

Only Butler could now change the course of events. Had he arranged for the four leading dissidents – Hailsham, Maudling, Macleod and himself – to confront Home as a group, it is doubtful if the latter could have prevailed. A meeting of the full Cabinet might also have convinced Home that there was insuperable opposition to his succession. But

Dilhorne refused to countenance such a meeting, an interesting commentary on the respective authority of the Lord Chancellor and the Deputy Prime Minister as well as further evidence of Dilhorne's less than impartial conduct during his time as self-appointed honest broker. On learning of the mounting opposition to him, Home's first inclination was to withdraw. Both Macmillan and Dilhorne sought to strengthen his resolve. The Cabinet cabal, it was claimed, was nothing but a collection of disappointed and over-ambitious colleagues. If Home gave in to such pressure, chaos would ensue and the Queen might even be obliged to send for the Leader of the Opposition to form a government – an inherently unlikely development granted the Conservatives' still sizeable majority in the House of Commons. Meanwhile, Powell sought to steel Butler into action. 'I said that if I were in Mr Butler's position, I would tell Lord Home that I, not he, enjoyed the confidence of the majority of the Cabinet ... and that it was I, not he, who would form the government.'[23] Not for the first time in his career, however, Butler displayed his particular flair for 'not rising to the occasion'.[24] Overlooked for the premiership in 1957, he perhaps no longer believed that the top job in British politics was destined to be his and now, presented with a loaded pistol, Butler declined to fire it.

Home wisely arranged to see existing members of the Cabinet individually. Their agreement to this was a tacit admission that the Foreign Secretary now held the initiative. Without strong leadership from Butler the opposition bloc soon collapsed. Hailsham was the first to throw in the towel and, although Butler and Maudling at first reserved their positions, they too agreed to serve under Home the following day, Saturday 19 October. In the end only Macleod and Powell refused office. Long-term antagonism probably determined Macleod's course. For Powell, who attached more importance than anyone else to Home's remark on 8 October that he would not be a candidate, there was a deep conviction that he was not the man for the job. 'Alec', he reportedly said, 'you know perfectly well that if I were to give you a different answer now I'd have to go home and turn all the mirrors round. I could never look at myself in the face again.'[25] For all that, shortly before lunch on 19 October 1963, the 14th Earl of Home kissed hands with the Queen on his appointment as Prime Minister and First Lord of the Treasury.

Part Two

THE LEADERSHIP

Chapter 4: Prime Minister (19 October 1963–16 October 1964)

Immediate reactions to the news were harsh. Under the headline 'Deplorable, Outrageous, Squalid', James Cameron in the *Sunday Mirror* argued that the processes of British democracy, long in decline, had now received 'the ultimate brush-off'. The *Observer* suggested that the Conservatives had had to settle for second-best and doubted whether Home had the perception or imagination for effective statesmanship in a rapidly changing world, while *The Times* drew attention to the new premier's lack of experience in home affairs and economics. The public and private statements of the Labour opposition are revealing. In public Wilson criticised the aristocratic cabal which had brought Home to power. 'In this ruthlessly competitive, scientific, technical, industrial age, a week of intrigues has produced a result based on family and hereditary connections ... After half a century of democratic advance, of social revolution ... the whole process has ground to a halt with a 14th Earl.'[1] But in private the Labour leader was ecstatic, seeing immediately how he could exploit the contrast between himself – a lower middle-class meritocrat – and the aristocratic Home to his party's advantage. Tony Benn made a similar point in the privacy of his diary. Home was 'a dud when it comes to exciting the electorate and Wilson will make rings round him'.[2] Perhaps more worryingly, discontent inside the Conservative Party seemed likely to rumble on. Criticising 'this last cruel blow' on the part of the Macmillan camp, Butler's Parliamentary Private Secretary seemed near to despair. 'How we can be expected in 1964 to go forward to victory under the 14th Earl of Home passes all understanding.'[3]

Home's immediate duty was to construct his government. His room for manoeuvre was extremely limited. Having first had to determine whether he could form an administration by finding out whether individual ministers were prepared to serve under him, he could not a few days later easily dispense with their services. Macleod's absence offered a convenient opening for the return of Selwyn Lloyd as Leader of the Commons; Powell's gave scope for the promotion to the Cabinet of Anthony Barber. John Hare became Party Chairman and was given a peerage as Lord Blakenham. Edward Heath took over an expanded and enhanced Board of Trade. Home's own elevation enabled Butler to assume the Foreign Secretaryship, some considerable compensation for his failure to secure the top prize. For the rest, Macmillan's Cabinet remained largely intact, albeit under new management. Home's next task was to ensure his own return to the House of Commons. Renouncing his peerage under the terms of the newly-enacted legislation, Home re-emerged as Sir Alec Douglas-Home and quickly found himself Conservative candidate for the forthcoming by-election at Kinross and West Perthshire where the existing Tory hopeful, the future Cabinet minister George Younger, was persuaded to stand aside. But for a fortnight after 23 October the Prime Minister held a seat in neither House of Parliament, a situation without parallel in modern British history. Douglas-Home waged a competent campaign in what was at the time a safe Conservative seat. He had no difficulty in relating to the electorate in this largely agricultural constituency and his speeches to small, sympathetic audiences were generally well received. It was, however, clear that he would need to work hard on economic issues and co-ordinate his approach with that of the Chancellor, Reginald Maudling. While the latter sounded a note of caution, warning on 26 October of the dangers of an inflationary spiral, Douglas-Home talked of a 4 per cent growth rate and campaigned with commitments for 400,000 new houses in a year together with vast expenditure on education and hospital building. Elected with a reduced but still satisfactory majority of more than 9,000 votes, he now returned to the House of Commons after an absence of 12 years.

'Obituary: The death occurred on October 18th, 1963 of the Conservative Party. The Conservative Party had been suffering from severe Macmillan for the last seven years and although this had finally cleared up, its condition was so debilitated as a result that a sudden attack of Lord Home caused its immediate demise.' Thus *Private Eye* magazine greeted the news of Lord Home's leadership. (From Richard Ingrams (ed), *The Life and Times of Private Eye* (Penguin Books Ltd, Harmondsworth: 1971) p 91.)

Douglas-Home's first performances as Prime Minister seemed to confirm some of the fears that had accompanied his appointment. His first television broadcast conveyed sincerity but failed to excite. His task, he suggested, was *to serve the nation. The second thing I would like to say to you is that you need expect no stunts from me, just plain straight talking.*[4] He was not a natural television performer and never achieved that rare capacity to use this medium to talk directly to the individual viewer. He appeared wooden and nothing could make him telegenic. He betrayed his nervousness by a tendency to let his tongue shoot out, like that of a lizard, to moisten his dry lips. All the efforts of make-up artists failed fully to disguise the cadaverous image of his skull. On occasions he seemed poorly briefed. Interviewed by Robin Day in February 1964, he insisted that the British economy had seldom been stronger, only to be effectively contradicted the following day by the publication of the worst ever trade figures. 'He simply didn't understand most of the questions,' judged Tony Benn. 'He is a real asset to us.'[5] But when not required to speak from a political brief, Douglas-Home could be more impressive. Called upon to pay tribute following the assassination of President Kennedy in November 1963, he spoke with dignity and sincerity. The contrast with Labour's deputy leader, George Brown, who claimed a hitherto unknown close friendship with the dead President and who was in all probability the worse for drink, could not have been more stark. At the Commons despatch box Douglas-Home made a faltering start. His first speech as Prime Minister was also the first he had ever made from the front bench in the Lower House, and he seemed ill-prepared for the very different atmosphere compared with that which existed in the Lords. The American ambassador gave a dispassionate assessment of his performance. 'He seemed strained, repetitive and was occasionally at a loss for a word, giving impression of not being thoroughly at home in economic and domestic sections of speech with which he began, his economic presentation seemed over-simplified. He compared poorly with Wilson's thorough command of subject, polish and fluency.'[6]

... you need expect no stunts from me, just plain straight talking.

DOUGLAS-HOME

The Tories' ability to compete with the Labour leader, especially with a general election on the horizon, was a vital consideration to which little attention appeared to have been paid in the selection of their new leader. Douglas-Home's initial experience as Prime Minister probably determined the strategy that was adopted for the rest of his premiership. William Deedes, the Minister without Portfolio charged with co-ordinating the government's publicity, soon realised that the new premier would not win a gladiatorial contest against Harold Wilson. Closer in style to Attlee than to Wilson, Douglas-Home was 'not a presidential candidate but a traditional parliamentary leader'.[7] Deedes urged him to limit his television and parliamentary appearances and it is striking that, as Prime Minister, he made only four major speeches to the House of Commons. The preferred alternative was a series of whistle-stop addresses by which he would make himself better known up and down the country, while avoiding the strained image which he presented on television and the danger of a parliamentary mauling at the hands of the Labour leader. Rather than competing with Wilson, Conservative Central Office strategists saw value in emphasising Sir Alec's differences. The contrast between what the satirical television programme *That Was the Week that Was* dubbed 'Smart Alec and Dull Alec' would not necessarily work in the former's favour. The hope, suggested Macmillan, was that Wilson would come to be seen as a bore or, better still, a crook. If Douglas-Home could not easily appeal to the aspiring lower middle-class voter targeted by Labour, his aristocratic charm had greater potential purchase among women and the more old-fashioned working classes, where deference was still a factor.

Early in the New Year, therefore, Douglas-Home embarked upon a strenuous series of regional tours to 'meet the people'. His message was that the Conservatives had a programme of modernisation, despite having been in government for 12 years, which would better serve the interests of the country than would the adoption of Labour's socialism. The exercise began disastrously. An address in Swansea – 'perhaps the worst speech ever made by a British Prime Minister' – was unbelievably bad. 'Scarcely one sentence corresponded to what appeared in the press release, and often he was quite incomprehensible.'[8] But Douglas-Home steadily improved. His speeches seldom inspired, but he could be both clever and witty. He was at his best when speaking on his chosen patch of foreign affairs and at his most vehement in his denunciation of Labour's declared policy to abandon Britain's independent nuclear deterrent. He had no trouble winning over the party faithful. One local agent recalled that 'he made a wonderfully favourable impression. Everybody commented on how genuinely friendly he was, and how he seemed interested in what people were saying.'[9] But with a less sympathetic audience he could still seem cold and remote, and it is open to question how successful he was in attracting the floating voter whose decision would settle the outcome of the election. Some may have been impressed to have a Prime Minister who had played first-class cricket. But, as John Ramsden tellingly puts it, 'it was exactly the type of elector who did not think that Eton against Harrow was really first-class cricket who was so hard for Sir Alec to reach'.[10]

The left-wing Labour MP Tony Benn (b. 1925) was the first to take advantage of the 1963 Peerage Act, allowing him to renounce his inherited title of Viscount Stansgate and remain in the Commons, as both Douglas-Home and Quintin Hogg were to do. He went on to serve as Minister of Technology in the Wilson governments of the 1960s, and was Secretary of State for Industry and for Energy in the 1970s. He challenged unsuccessfully for the party leadership in 1988 and retired from the Commons in 2001 'to devote more time to politics'.

Macmillan's Cabinet was not Douglas-Home's only inheritance from his predecessor. The new government also continued with a legislative agenda that was already in place. Macmillan, too, had taken charge when the Conservative party was at a low ebb following the traumatic experience of Suez, but he at least had had plenty of time to shape the administration in his own image. Even if Douglas-Home had been inclined to strike out in new directions, the opportunity to do so did not exist. Indeed, the whole of his year-long premiership was dominated by the forthcoming election, a point he emphasised in his speech at Church House, Westminster, after his formal adoption as Conservative leader on 11 November. *From this moment on*, he declared, *the fact that there is a general election ahead of us must never be out of our minds. Every act that we take, every attitude that we strike, every speech that we make in Parliament or elsewhere, must have that in mind, because the one thing that matters is that this country should be saved from Socialism and that a Conservative Government should be returned.*[11]

> *... the one thing that matters is that this country should be saved from Socialism and that a Conservative Government should be returned.*
>
> DOUGLAS-HOME

The suggestion, first made by Macleod and repeated in various forms on several occasions since, that under Douglas-Home the Conservatives were 'for the first time since Bonar Law ... being led from the right of centre', is therefore of dubious relevance.[12] By this stage in its evolution the Tory party was firmly entrenched in the centre ground of the post-war consensus, its policies in the early 1960s more interventionist, corporatist indeed, than ever before or since. Douglas-Home as Prime Minister did nothing to change this. *All our policies had been put into place*, he later recalled, *and ... there was nothing to do.*[13] The new premier's instincts may have been less interventionist and more sceptical about ever higher levels of government expenditure, but he became nonetheless the somewhat unlikely champion of policies that differed more in rhetoric than in substance from those proposed by Labour. We have only tantalising glimpses of the direction in which, given time, an unfettered Douglas-Home premiership might have led. Asked by Michael Fraser of the Conservative Central Office to distil his political philosophy into a paper which he drew up over the Christmas recess, the Prime Minister revealed a leaning towards a form of right-wing aristocratic paternalism which would not have been well received by most of his senior colleagues. In a tract peppered with sporting metaphors, Douglas-Home wrote of a half-educated electorate and suggested that countrymen, living close to nature, had a sixth sense about what is possible or impossible. But these were gut feelings rather than part of a coherent political philosophy. Indeed, on another occasion he defined his brand of Conservatism simply in terms of *doing the right thing at the right time*.[14]

There were, then, few surprises in the new government's legislative programme. The hastily-prepared Queen's Speech sought to pick up the agenda of the Macmillan years, maintaining the overall principle of the need to modernise the country's institutions and practices. Typical was the decision to accept the Robbins Report on Higher Education, published less than a week into the new premiership. Its key idea was that all students qualified by ability and attainment to go to a university or college should be able to do so, and it thus set in train a massive expansion in higher education. Only one new measure stood out as being other than tidying up the unfinished business of the previous administration. This was a bill to abolish Retail Price Maintenance (RPM). It had much intrinsic merit, removing a distortion in the market and opening up the prospect of cheaper prices through increased competition. But the timing of the measure was curious. As RPM would not come to an end before the next election, the gratitude of consumers for lower prices would not be apparent to outweigh the damage done to around half a million small retailers, most of whom were thought to be Conservative supporters. Significantly, Macmillan, Macleod and Maudling had already given consideration to such a measure and had concluded that it would be unwise to risk alienating otherwise reliable voters in the run-up to an election.

The issue caused considerable dissension within both the Cabinet and the parliamentary party. Lloyd, Hogg (Hailsham), Maudling and Butler were all opposed, while Redmayne suggested that 'we should concentrate on short-term politics and remember that small traders are natural Conservative voters'.[15] But the bill had a determined champion in Edward Heath, who argued that it was the best way of dispelling the image of a tired government that had been in power too long and of convincing the electorate that the party remained a dynamic, modernising force. Showing something of the stubbornness that would become a trademark of his later career, the President of the Board of Trade set his face against compromises which would have excluded certain commodities from the scope of the bill. In the end it was the Prime Minister's backing for Heath, despite serious reservations, which carried the day. After three hours of Cabinet discussions the critics had to admit defeat. In the Commons, however, over 40 Tory MPs either voted against the measure or abstained, the largest show of dissent since the fall of Neville Chamberlain in May 1940. Overall, the bill, whatever its merits, proved unnecessarily divisive and, granted the narrow margin between victory and defeat at the general election, may even have been responsible for Douglas-Home's loss of office. A

Prime Minister with a surer touch on the home front might have avoided this issue and begun instead to tackle the problem of industrial relations, where there was a growing Conservative consensus in opposition to unofficial and 'wild-cat' strikes.

If the Douglas-Home premiership brought little in the way of new policies, his style of government did see a marked change of direction. His approach was much less presidential than that of his predecessor and he had no desire to keep every aspect of government policy within his personal control. He 'left his Ministers to get on with the job, and to come to him on their own initiative if they needed help'.[16] A natural devolver, he made no pretence to having expertise in areas where his ministers were altogether better qualified. Nowhere was this more apparent than in the management of the economy. Interviewed by Kenneth Harris a year before becoming Prime Minister, Douglas-Home had mocked his own credentials for the top job in British politics with words which would haunt him during his 12 months in Downing Street. *When I have to read economic documents I have to have a box of matches and start moving them into position to simplify and illustrate the points to myself.*[17] Not surprisingly, he broke with recent precedent and declined to chair the Cabinet's Economic Policy Committee. But his problem was that economics dominated both his premiership and the run-up to the election, with Wilson skilfully convincing the electorate that the country's affairs were being mismanaged and that Labour offered the path to economic salvation. More generally, the Labour leader himself dominated the Douglas-Home premiership in a manner

When I have to read economic documents I have to have a box of matches and start moving them into position to simplify and illustrate the points to myself.

DOUGLAS-HOME

The Special Relationship

Preparing for Douglas-Home's visit to Washington in February 1964, President Johnson's advisers drew attention to an essential truth about the so-called Special Relationship. Whereas the 'close US-UK association [was] the most important single factor in British foreign policy', for Americans Britain's friendship was valuable but not pre-eminent. In short, the relationship was more special for Britain than it was for the United States. There had been a time, as recently as the early stages of the Second World War, when Britain could speak to the United States on a basis of something approaching equality. But that moment had soon passed. As the Americans fully mobilised their war effort, Britain was left far behind. What Keith Sainsbury has described as the 'turning point' was reached by the time of the conference at Tehran in 1943. In the post-war world the United States would be in a different league of superpowers from Britain, even though the latter retained interests and influence in most parts of the world.

But British policy-makers found it difficult to reconcile themselves to the change in the balance of the relationship. Indeed, they saw the American partnership as a means to enable Britain to punch above its weight in the world arena. Not surprisingly, successive American presidents tended to find the British attitude tiresome – an unrealistic attempt to turn back the clock to an era that had passed by. Indeed, they expected to be able to dictate policy to the junior partner in the alliance. So Johnson's advisers reminded him of specific grievances against Britain, especially its continuing determination to trade with communist Cuba. More generally, Washington felt that long-term credits to communist countries were depriving the West of a useful weapon in the on-going Cold War. The Americans were also irritated by the stress which Douglas-Home placed on the supposed 'independence' of the British nuclear deterrent.

Occasionally, the close personal relationship between the President and the Prime Minister can partially conceal the reality of the Anglo-American relationship. But sentiment played little part in Johnson's attitude towards the British premier in 1964.

achieved by very few leaders of the opposition. In the last resort Douglas-Home never fully succeeded in counteracting Wilson's propaganda offensive of youthful dynamism in contrast to his own supposed reactionary irrelevance.

As Cabinet chairman Douglas-Home was brisk, methodical and, once he had made up his mind on an issue, decisive. His style was not dissimilar to that of Clement Attlee and, like Attlee, he could be intolerant of ministers whose own contributions to debate he deemed verbose. Reginald Maudling was one of those who enjoyed working for him – 'he was a man for whom one could feel respect and under whose leadership one could give one's full efforts'.[18] Civil servants found him kind and courteous and appreciated his ability to come to a decision. He was able to put people at ease and to inspire affection, while his informality was natural and not contrived. He was genuinely interested in the procedures of government and saw scope for significant reform. He was keen on the idea of streamlining the system of Cabinet government and relying on a series of strategic committees at which most important decisions would be taken. This vision, very much in line with developments that have occurred over the last 25 years, could not be implemented in the short time available to him, but Douglas-Home, in the event of a fourth Conservative election victory,

Lyndon Baines Johnson (1908–73) was Kennedy's Vice President and was sworn in as his successor on board Air Force One after his assassination in Dallas on 22 November 1963. Johnson's personal interest was in domestic affairs and combating poverty (the 'Great Society'), but he inherited Kennedy's war in Vietnam which escalated after the Gulf of Tonkin incident in 1964, until by 1968 it dominated his presidency ('Hey, Hey, LBJ, How Many Kids did you Kill Today?'). That year he announced he would not stand for re-election.

had planned to reinstate Enoch Powell to high office with a brief to cut back on the workload of the full Cabinet.

Only occasionally did issues of foreign affairs allow him to set the political agenda on the basis of his known field of expertise. A visit to Washington in February 1964 for talks with President Johnson was only partially successful. Though the prevailing atmosphere was friendly enough, there was tension behind the scenes over Britain's decision not to block the sale of British Leyland buses to Cuba and the resulting communiqué between the two leaders was no more than anodyne. The Rhodesian problem remained unresolved and, while Douglas-Home succeeded in maintaining cordial relations with the white regime in Salisbury, which believed him keen to reach a face-saving settlement, there is no real evidence that he would have been able to avoid the unilateral declaration of independence which greeted Harold Wilson's Labour government in November 1965. By the summer of 1964 problems in Cyprus, Vietnam, Malaysia and Aden gave him some scope to display his knowledge of foreign affairs and in July he presided effectively over the Commonwealth Prime Ministers' Conference. For the most part, however, the battle between the parties was fought out over issues where Douglas-Home felt least at ease. It is revealing that one Cabinet minister soon decided that, even in the event of a Conservative election victory, Douglas-Home would need to be advised by 'some sort of "Herbert Morrison" figure with an oversight of domestic policy'.[19] Maudling's 1964 Budget made significant increases in indirect taxation, but his 'dash for growth' represented a huge gamble for both the country and the Conservative Party. Government spending plans were running above the figure that the country could afford, even assuming that the optimistic target of a 4 per cent growth rate could be met.

The most important decision of the Douglas-Home premiership related to the timing of the general election. Unlike James Callaghan in 1978–9, it cannot be said that he got it wrong for at no date earlier than that chosen in October 1964 would the Conservatives have been more likely to have won. During the first six months of his leadership the Conservatives were consistently behind Labour in the opinion polls. During the premiership as a whole, Wilson's approval rating never fell below 61 per cent, while Douglas-Home's never exceeded 48 per cent. An NOP poll in April found that 71 per cent of the electorate thought the Labour leader to be 'brilliant' and 80 per cent 'tough'. The corresponding figures for the Prime Minister were just 53 and 54 per cent. Maudling pressed for an early election, a sign perhaps that he anticipated trouble before long over the economy, but the Prime Minster accepted the advice of Central Office that such a step would be electoral suicide. On 9 April, the day of elections to the Greater London Council, Douglas-Home declared that the general election would be held in the autumn. When heavy Conservative defeats were announced later that day, it was clear that he had made the right decision. Over the summer months the relative standing of the two leaders in the polls hardly changed, but that of their parties did. An advertising campaign which stressed the country's rising standard of living appeared to be bearing fruit with Conservative support finally starting to rise. A recovery was already discernible in the borough council elections in May and that same month the government held off the Liberal challenge in a by-election in Devizes. Meanwhile Sir Alec himself was growing in confidence. His performance at Prime Minister's Questions in the Commons displayed increasing sure-footedness. Outside Parliament his speeches on foreign affairs afforded him greater plausibility as Prime Minister. In August and September the

Tories were actually ahead of Labour according to NOP. On 27 September Gallup put them in the lead for the first time for three years. The *Sunday Times*, which had not supported him hitherto, was forced to concede that it was Sir Alec himself who had transformed the Conservatives' prospects through his honesty and integrity, establishing in the process a reassuring image of trust reminiscent of Stanley Baldwin 30 years before.

Polling day was fixed for Thursday 15 October, almost the last date that was legally open to him. It was never going to be an easy election for Douglas-Home to win. The Conservatives, it is true, could point to some impressive statistics on advancing living standards. There were now four times as many cars on the road as in 1951. The number of televisions had increased 13-fold over the same period. The number of children staying on at school beyond the statutory age of 15 had nearly doubled, while university places, even without Robbins, had already increased by 60 per cent. Against all this, however, was a strong feeling that the country was still not performing as well as it should and a deep conviction that, after 13 years of Tory government, it was now time for a change. Wilson exploited the prevailing mood with consummate skill. Moreover, Sir Alec was an inherently unlikely standard-bearer for the Conservatives' claim that they were better equipped than Labour to carry forward the modernising agenda that the country needed. He would not have wished to compete with Wilson in slogans about the white-heat of the technological revolution. Even so, his grouse-moor image seemed curiously out-of-step with the youth culture of the mid-1960s. As one disillusioned voter had put it shortly after Douglas-Home became Prime Minister: 'We are sick of seeing old-looking men dressed in flat caps and bedraggled tweeds strolling with a twelve-bore. For God's sake, what is your campaign manager doing? These photographs of Macmillan's ghost with Home's face date about 1912.'[20]

Douglas-Home's campaign did not get off to a good start. In his adoption speech in his constituency he referred prematurely to the 'socialist government' and suggested that Labour's plans for steel would involve the nationalisation of a manufacturing industry for the first time. In fact, Attlee's government had already nationalised steel once, only for Churchill's administration to return it to the private sector. Worse was to follow. Appearing on the television programme *Election Forum*, and looking 'so exhausted that his skin appeared to be drawn tightly over his skull',[21] he referred to old-age pensions as 'donations'. This one word seemed to encapsulate just how remote the Prime Minister was from the lives of ordinary voters. It was, his biographer suggests, 'probably the worst mistake of his entire premiership' and it was certainly exploited ruthlessly by Labour spokesmen for the remainder of the campaign.[22] Thereafter, he embarked on a nationwide speaking tour, leaving the campaign in London, and particularly on television, largely in the hands of Heath and Maudling. The idea was to stress that, in contrast to Labour's one-man band, the Conservatives were a team which could bat right down to number 11. But one consequence was to leave Sir Alec somewhat marginalised at a time when the 'presidential' factor was becoming more important in British elections. Up and down the country he did and said little that was memorable and, as the authors of the Nuffield study of the election concede, seldom can a Prime Minister's words have attracted less attention. His one television broadcast was not a success. It was, felt *The Times*, 'a symphony in black and white delivered by a tone-deaf pianist for, though the notes were all there and in the right order, the performance was so totally lacking in style and emotion that its impact was lost on the ear'.[23]

In his public speeches Douglas-Home defied advice and focused on the claim that Labour's declared intention to give up the country's nuclear deterrent made it unfit to govern. In one sense this was a wise move, allowing him to concentrate on issues about which he felt both confident and passionate. But his problem was that his own convictions on this question failed to resonate with the electors. Only 4 per cent of the postcards sent in to the BBC's *Election Forum* had been about defence, while just 13 per cent of an NOP sample placed the deterrent on their list of most important issues. This was not the way the election would be won. Overall, the Prime Minister waged a negative campaign with an emphasis on the dangers inherent in Labour's programme rather than setting out a renewed Conservative agenda for the years ahead. When he did try to trail new Tory policies, the effect was not always what he had intended. He stressed his party's desire to end restrictive practices in industrial relations and to have an agreed incomes policy, but in a press conference on 3 October came near to implying compulsion if the trade unions refused to co-operate. One speech in Bradford a few days later caught the national attention. In it the Prime Minister suggested that the government's Commonwealth Immigration Act of 1962 had prevented perhaps a million more immigrants from *flooding* into the country.

'I will make my speech. I may inform you it is my own speech. I wrote it myself, and I can read it, and I understand what it means when I have read it.'

HAROLD WILSON

Warning of the consequences for employment, housing and education, he gave an assurance that a new Conservative government would keep the number of permits under review and strengthen the safeguards against evasion.

Europe

Some of the advocates of European unity have supported a federal system for Europe. This has caused a good deal of anxiety, not least to my right hon. Friend the Member for Wolverhampton South-West (Mr. Powell). Some may still like and pursue the idea.

What has happened within the partnership of the Six? Political change, it is agreed, has to be unanimous. On all important matters they have found that they must proceed by consensus. That is the experience after ten years of practice in the Community.

The reason is clear. Great countries with the history of the European nations cannot be dragooned or coerced into a pattern of political association which one or the other of them does not like. The attempt would be folly. It would break up the Community. Even to try to do such a thing is totally against the spirit of the association. Decisions on the political evolution of the Community are not for now, even for tomorrow, but for the future. Any decision made on political advance must have the unanimous support of all the members of the partnership.

All the way through our history events in the centre and west of Europe have conditioned our foreign policy. The balance of power is achieved through a European contribution, and the omens that the Western Europeans will have to carry a greater share of the responsibility for Western defence ... are ... stronger than they have been since the war.

I am not one of those who believe that the United States will ever desert Europe ... Nevertheless, the chances are that ... the future will have to be organised with a more distinctively European contribution, embracing within it the strength of France. It will take time, and it will take great patience, to work out the designs, but when Germany, France, Italy and the rest sit down to talk about their problems of security and their attitude to world problems, I use the word in the most accurate sense when I say that it is vital that we should be in their councils.

[Douglas-Home in the House of Commons 21 October 1971]

Where Sir Alec was at his most vulnerable was in dealing with hecklers. With an invited, all-ticket audience, and especially if speaking on issues of his choice, he could give a competent performance. But, interrupted by a hostile crowd, he tended to go to pieces. Labour activists did their best to discomfort him by making sure that his speeches were peppered with interventions from off-stage. In such situations Douglas-Home appeared stiff and prim. He lacked Wilson's capacity – or that of Macleod and Hogg on his own side – to react on his feet and turn such occasions to his own advantage. A speech in Birmingham's indoor Rag Market on 8 October proved disastrous. The sight on television of the British Prime Minister being drowned out by an element in the crowd left a lasting impression. For Lord Blakenham, the Party Chairman, it was the turning point of the whole campaign with no real opportunity thereafter to turn things round. *Up till then he thought we were winning*, recalled Sir Alec. *After that the advantage began to slide away*.[24] In marked contrast, Wilson was able to charm an audience in the same forbidding arena with his unique combination of wit and platform skill, and to do so largely at his rival's expense. 'I will make my speech. I may inform you it *is* my own speech. I wrote it myself, and I can read it, and I understand what it means when I have read it.'[25]

During the second half of the campaign Labour wisely shifted the emphasis of its attack on to the government's management of the economy. Balance of payments figures published on 30 September showed a worrying deficit of £73 million. Wilson compared the Prime Minister with John Bloom, the slick but rather suspect entrepreneur whose Rolls Razor business had recently collapsed. Meanwhile, George Brown suggested that the country was lurching towards the biggest economic crisis since the war. 'If the present trend continues,' he warned, 'it will mean that our jobs, our wages, our hire purchase agreements, our mortgage rates are all in jeopardy.'[26] Such had been the government's uncertain handling of economic affairs since around 1962 – the era of 'stop, go' – that it was relatively easy to plant the idea that the supposed recovery was only superficial and that a Conservative victory would be followed, as before, by renewed policies of deflation.

Conservative optimism began once more to wane. Characteristically, Butler expressed his misgivings in public. 'Things might start slipping in the last few days', he told George Gale of the *Daily Express*. But 'they won't slip towards us'.[27] In the event, the result was agonisingly close. Early declarations from largely urban constituencies suggested a comfortable Labour victory. Overnight, however, as results came in from the shires, the Conservatives regained much ground and, for a while, a narrow Tory victory seemed possible. But, by the afternoon of 16 October, it was clear that Labour would have a small overall majority. The final result was Labour 317, Conservatives and their allies 304, Liberals 9, giving Harold Wilson a majority of just four seats, or five if the Conservative Speaker's position was taken into account.

> **George Brown** (1914–85) was a trade union official turned Labour MP who was Deputy Leader of the party from 1960 to 1970. Beaten for the leadership by Wilson in 1963, he was head of Wilson's Department of Economic Affairs in 1964, and Foreign Secretary from 1966–8. His political career was marred by his heavy drinking (*Private Eye* coined the phrase 'tired and emotional' as a euphemism for his behaviour), and he lost his seat in the 1970 election. Ennobled as Baron George-Brown, he joined the SDP in 1981 but made no contribution to it before his death in 1985.

Granted the close outcome, how well had Sir Alec actually done? It was calculated that it would only have taken a few hundred extra Conservative votes, distributed judiciously in key marginal seats, to have kept the government in office. Others suggested that, had the election been delayed for a week or two, the news of Khrushchev's fall from power in Russia and the simultaneous explosion of a nuclear weapon in China might have shifted the priorities of enough electors to make the necessary differ-ence. Any one of a number of factors could, in the circum-stances, be held up as being of critical importance – Heath's insistence on abolishing RPM; the continuing rumblings of discontent associated with

I think that the 13 years was just too much and the public were a bit bored with both the parties who had claimed the centre of the stage for so long and, being the government, we got the worst of it.

DOUGLAS-HOME

Powell and, more particularly, Macleod; Butler's indiscre-tion during the campaign; Maudling's failure to prosecute the government's economic case with sufficient vigour; or Hogg's unnecessary outburst about the possibility of adul-terers on Labour's front bench. Seen in this light Douglas-Home's achievement was indeed remarkable. He had rescued his party from the depths of despair in 1963, put at least a strong sticking plaster over the wounds of the Profumo affair, restored a degree of unity to the party's ranks and come ago-nisingly close to a record fourth successive election victory.

Yet a very different interpretation may also be offered. This was in fact a poor result for the Conservatives, partially concealed only because Labour failed significantly to improve on their performance in 1959. The Conservative share of the vote had dropped by as much as 6 per cent, the largest fall experienced between elections by any party since the Tory debacle of 1945. And if the narrowness of the defeat encouraged the quest for scapegoats who had deprived Douglas-Home of an historic victory, it was equally possible to suggest that another Prime Minister with wider appeal and greater electoral skills – Butler, Hogg (assuming no personal gaffes) or even Macmillan himself – would surely have achieved success. Douglas-Home's own assessment was characteristically down-to-earth and not without its merits. *I think that the 13 years was just too much and the public were a bit bored with both the parties who had claimed the centre of the stage for so long and, being the government, we got the worst of it.*[28] For all that, after just 363 days, Alec Douglas-Home's premiership was at an end.

Part Three

THE LEGACY

Chapter 5: After Number 10 (1964–95)

Recent history suggests that the loss of a general election must now lead inevitably to the resignation of a Conservative leader. It was not always so. Both Baldwin and Churchill fought back from reversals at the polls to head later governments. While Arthur Balfour never again secured the premiership, he remained Conservative leader for nearly six years after the loss of the 1906 election. Alec Douglas-Home's mood in October 1964 was relatively buoyant. Initial disappointment at the loss of office was soon overcome by a sense of achievement deriving from the narrowness of Labour's victory. Douglas-Home, it was widely thought, had performed wonders in restoring party morale after the deep depression that had characterised Macmillan's final year and in leading a largely reunited party to the very brink of what would have been an historic fourth successive electoral triumph. Even the rebels of the previous October, Macleod and Powell, were now willing to join the Shadow Cabinet under Douglas-Home's leadership. Furthermore, the narrowness of Labour's victory meant that another general election might be called at any time and the last thing the Tories needed was to be caught off-guard in the middle of a possibly divisive contest for the succession. An opinion poll suggested that 56 per cent of Tory voters wanted Douglas-Home to remain and even those MPs who thought that they would do better under a new leader were reluctant to force the issue, such was the feeling of respect and affection which the present incumbent now enjoyed.

Yet it soon became clear that his talents were ill-suited to the role of Leader of the Opposition. He began well enough, telling the Commons that it was not the Conservatives' intention to exploit the parliamentary situation in a way that would make good government impossible. Harold Wilson noted a 'delightful blend of the sardonic and the serious'. Douglas-Home 'ribbed me ... about the size of the Government [and] described some of the senior appointments as having been based on the demobilisation formula, "age and length of service"', a not inappropriate comment on some of the deadwood which found its way into Labour's Cabinet.[1] It was not long, however, before the mood began to change. Douglas-Home was ready to be a statesman, but the party, or at least sections of it, were looking for something different – someone who would take advantage of the government's problems, hit hard and if necessary low, and remove Labour from power as quickly as possible. Iain Macleod was soon pressing the Shadow Cabinet to organise a more combative opposition than the leader seemed to want. Douglas-Home was never one for knock-about politics and was seldom the new Prime Minister's equal in the cut-and-thrust of parliamentary debate. He even came off worst in an early encounter on his own preferred ground, in arguing with Wilson as to the reality of the so-called independent nuclear deterrent. As early as January, Labour's assiduous diarist, Richard Crossman, was noting that, while Douglas-Home was an 'amiable, pleasant figure', he was 'totally ineffective as Leader of the Opposition; and already there are ostentatious to-ings and fro-ings about who shall replace him and how it shall be done'.[2] Above all, the Labour government would be judged by its management of the economy and Douglas-Home lacked the expertise to lead an effective critique of its performance.

Yet the months before his resignation were not without achievement. He initiated a wide-ranging review of party policy under the direction of Edward Heath. In March 1965 the Shadow Cabinet reiterated the intention to seek entry into the EEC and accepted the need to educate the party, the farming sector and the Commonwealth about the need to follow such a course. The appointment of a new, young Party Chairman, Edward DuCann, in January seemed to mark a clean break with the 'grouse moor' image of which critics complained. Above all, Douglas-Home redeemed a pledge, made while in government, by setting up a committee to review the procedure for changing the party leader. As *The Times* put it, any new system had to be capable of conferring legitimacy. 'The customary processes of consultation are widely thought to be unrepeatable after the events of October 1963.'[3] This committee brought together several leading protagonists of the earlier drama – Butler, Hogg, Macleod, Dilhorne, Redmayne and Douglas-Home himself. Its report, adopted early in 1965, allowed for a simple process of election by Conservative MPs. With hindsight, Douglas-Home might have been well advised to submit himself immediately to the new procedure. His failure to do so meant that, in many minds, he continued to lack that legitimacy to which *The Times* had referred.

There were also a few indications of Douglas-Home's inclination to shift the party's centre of gravity to the right, for which his brief months as Prime Minister had afforded few opportunities. He had stopped short of repudiating Peter Griffiths, the Conservatives' victorious general election candidate at Smethwick following an overtly racist campaign. Now, with Peter Thorneycroft appointed Shadow Home

Secretary and Enoch Powell raising the subject in a series of speeches, it was clear that the party was ready to take up the issue of Commonwealth immigration. After one Powell speech Douglas-Home wrote to express his entire agreement and he himself turned to this theme in an address in Hampstead on 3 February. It was an important statement of party policy. *We also believe that we should have the power to assist voluntary repatriation and that the dependants must be counted against the limits on numbers and that the total should be further reduced.*[4]

Infamous for his so-called 'Rivers of Blood' speech in Birmingham on 20 April 1968, John Enoch Powell (1912–98) had resigned from Macmillan's government over increased public expenditure in 1958, but had returned as Health Secretary in 1960. He was defence spokesman in Heath's Shadow Cabinet, but was sacked after making his speech attacking uncontrolled immigration. Strongly opposed to Britain's entry into the EEC, he advised voters to vote Labour in 1974 as they promised a referendum on the issue. He then left the Conservatives and joined the Ulster Unionists, sitting for South Down until 1987.

As yet, however, immigration was not the issue to set the Conservative Party alight. As 1965 proceeded, criticism of Douglas-Home's performance slowly increased. *Factious opposition does not come easily to me*, he privately complained, *but is that what the country wants?*[5] After 13 years in power the party was impatient at its removal from office. A surprise victory over the government in a by-election at Leyton was soon over-shadowed by the loss to the Liberals in March of the seat of Roxburgh, Selkirk and Peebles, dangerously close to the leader's own aristocratic base. Douglas-Home himself raised the question of the leadership at the Shadow Cabinet, calling for his colleagues' unanimous and wholehearted support, but Macleod was one who argued that the party was still not making enough impact. In the *Spectator* Alan Watkins drew over-dramatic parallels with the situation that prevailed before the abdication crisis of 1936. Everyone knew that something was wrong, but no-one was prepared to say so openly. Who now would fill the role played then by the Bishop of Bradford? Selwyn Lloyd wrote privately that, despite 'quite a lot of snarling about Alec', no potential successor was making any particular mark.[6] But this was not the case. By making Heath rather than Maudling Shadow Chancellor, Douglas-Home had offered the former the opportunity to convince the party that he was the man to beat Wilson at his own game. In this the Conservatives were mistaken. Though he would defeat Wilson at the 1970 general election, Heath was seldom the Labour leader's equal as a political operator. Nonetheless, some good performances in the Commons converted someone who had scarcely been considered in 1963 into a serious contender for the succession 18 months later. Though Heath himself stood aloof, his supporters, with or without his encourage-

Factious opposition does not come easily to me, but is that what the country wants?

DOUGLAS-HOME

ment, began to canvass his claims. Meanwhile, with trouble brewing on Labour's backbenches at the prospect of a bill to renationalise steel, Crossman concluded that it was only the 'reluctance of the country to go back to the inadequacies of Alec Douglas-Home' that sustained the government in power.[7]

It was Harold Wilson who took the decisive step. His announcement on 16 June that there would be no general election in 1965 removed from Douglas-Home the protective fear which had ensured his position so far. A new leader would now have plenty of time to settle in before the country next went to the polls. The *Sunday Express* and *Daily Telegraph* soon ran stories of movements to oust the incumbent, but Douglas-Home himself told a press conference in Hull of his intention to carry on. The matter was raised at a meeting of the executive of the 1922 Committee in early July when it became clear that 25 backbench MPs had requested a debate on the leadership. The chairman, Sir William Anstruther-Gray, succeeded temporarily in defusing the situation by agreeing to report the disquiet felt to the leader, but this did not prevent *The Times* from writing of an 'attempted putsch'. On 18 July an article appeared in the *Sunday Times* under the name of William Rees-Mogg, entitled 'The Right Moment to Change'. Couched in cricketing metaphors which Douglas-Home would have appreciated, it suggested that the leader had played a 'captain's innings', but that the time had now come for a younger man to take his place. If that were not enough, a National Opinion Poll seemed to undermine his one remaining argument for staying on. It suggested that twice as many people believed Wilson to be 'pleasant' as thought he was and, astonishingly, that more people regarded the Prime Minister than the Opposition Leader as 'straight' and 'sincere'. Meanwhile, Labour's lead in the polls had increased to 4.6 per cent.

By the time of his appearance before the 1922 Committee on 22 July, Douglas-Home had decided that the game was up. He was 'obviously tired, depressed and determined to go. I was alone with him for half an hour', recalled John Boyd-Carpenter. 'But I could not move him from his intention.'[8] With dignity and without histrionics Douglas-Home read out a statement announcing that he would resign. His sensitivity and pride would not permit him to outstay his welcome. Having served eight years as a Cabinet minister and a further 12 months at Number 10, he was not prepared to fight to retain a position which in any case held few attractions for him. As one who worked closely with him at this time later put it, 'when there was so much bitching about him ... he decided to pack it in and stand down'.[9] His own brother was more blunt. 'Suicide' may have been on Sir Alec's death certificate, but it was 'murder none the less'.[10]

Yet Douglas-Home was not dead, even in the political sense. He was now 62 years of age and could easily have retired with dignity. There was an argument that it would have been better for the party had he held on. Labour was likely to win the next general election, if only because the electorate wanted to give it a fair chance and, by resigning when he did, Douglas-Home was effectively saddling his successor with the stigma of defeat. But this was largely wisdom after the event. Douglas-Home had had enough, at least of the leadership. Yet politics always held a greater attraction for him than he tended to imply and his career on the front bench still had almost a decade to run. In the manner of his departure from the leadership the closest recent parallel was with Arthur Balfour in 1911. The latter had also been the object of a mounting chorus of criticism over his too gentlemanly conduct of opposition politics which left him disinclined to carry on. But, like Balfour too, Douglas-Home could still look forward to a further period of government office. Balfour re-emerged as Foreign Secretary under Lloyd George at the height of the Great War in 1916 and was still a Cabinet minister as late as 1929, shortly before his death. Douglas-Home was unique among post-war Prime Ministers in agreeing to serve under his successor as party leader and in later occupying another Cabinet post.

After, somewhat surprisingly, defeating Reginald Maudling in the contest for the succession, Edward Heath invited Douglas-Home to join his Shadow Cabinet with overall responsibility for foreign affairs. He accepted and held this position throughout the succeeding years of opposition. Though he never numbered among Heath's inner circle, he enjoyed the new leader's confidence while securing a position of unique affection among the party's ranks to which he had never before aspired. Imperceptibly, he transmogrified into a much-respected elder statesman. Furthermore, for the rest of his life he set an example of public loyalty to whoever held the Conservative leadership which not all of his successors found it easy to follow. The transformation in his position was evident in the rapturous reception he was accorded at the Conservative Party Conference that autumn. But he again found himself at the centre of a political storm. The white government in Rhodesia was clearly moving towards a unilateral and illegal declaration of independence and it fell to Douglas-Home to argue against a vote in opposition to sanctions being imposed in such an eventuality. It was a difficult task, not least because he was personally doubtful about the efficacy of sanctions and because he felt some qualified sympathy for the regime of Ian Smith in Salisbury. UDI created 'a crisis for the governing party which was even more dangerous to the opposition'.[11] But on this occasion, and at successive party conferences over the following years, Douglas-Home carried the day and succeeded in maintaining a broadly bi-partisan approach to the Rhodesian problem against the clamour of the Tory right led by figures such as Lord Salisbury and Duncan Sandys. It is doubtful if any other figure could have held the line. His own view remained what it had been when, as Commonwealth Secretary, he had grappled with an earlier phase of the same issue. *Majority rule in Rhodesia today or tomorrow would bring collapse and ruin.*[12]

Heath's years as Leader of the Opposition were in some respects over-shadowed by the looming presence of Enoch Powell, sacked as shadow spokesman on defence following an inflammatory speech on race relations delivered in Birmingham in April 1968. Douglas-Home would not have used anything like Powell's language, but he felt a lingering sympathy for some of his sentiments and had himself made several speeches that year calling for the number of immigrants to be strictly limited. In any case Douglas-Home never lost his respect for Powell's formidable intellect and he was the only member of the Shadow Cabinet not to shun Powell when the latter made his first appearance at Westminster following the 'rivers of blood' speech. As late as 1971 he told Powell to carry on making speeches on immigration *because that is so vitally important and you are so right about it*.[13] In other respects Powell was putting himself forward as an early champion of a form of free-market Conservatism that would come into its own under the leadership of Margaret Thatcher. Douglas-Home, though not prominent in this debate, gave further occasional evidence of his right-wing credentials. In 1969 he told the Monday Club that *the best government was the least government*, a sentiment that ran counter to the broad thrust of party thinking since 1945.[14]

On other questions he showed a more liberal strain, quietly regretting, for example, the collapse of the Labour government's attempt to reform the House of Lords. In May 1968 Heath surprised Scottish Conservatives by raising the possibility of a Scottish Assembly. Against a background of mounting nationalism, Douglas-Home was asked to chair a committee of enquiry into the possibility of further devolution for Scotland. Its report, *Scotland's Government*, proposed a 'Scottish Convention' to be directly elected at the time of parliamentary elections. With no ministerial boxes to detain him, Douglas-Home even had time to pursue interests outside party politics. But his term as President of the MCC in 1966–7, which saw the beginnings of what became known as the

D'Oliveira affair, when the South African authorities seemed to have applied pressure to exclude a mixed-race cricketer from the English touring team, offered less scope for relaxation than might have been anticipated.

For much of this period a Conservative victory at the next general election seemed inevitable, though Heath never fulfilled the hopes of his enthusiastic supporters and his personal popularity consistently lagged behind that of his party. Wilson's touch never fully returned after the devaluation of the pound in 1967. By 1970, however, there were clear signs that Labour was once more in the ascendant and leading Conservatives braced themselves for a third successive electoral defeat. In such an eventuality Heath's position as leader would be untenable, leaving Powell well placed to seize his crown. Senior Tories prepared to draft Douglas-Home to return to the leadership, even for a limited period, as the only figure capable of blocking Powell.

In the event this scenario did not arise. Heath confounded the polls (and just about everyone but himself) by securing a comfortable working majority of 30 seats when the country voted in June. So unexpected was the result that some pundits ascribed Wilson's defeat to public disenchantment following England's defeat in the football World Cup. It was widely recognised that Douglas-Home could hardly be denied a return to the Foreign Office if he so wished it. Maudling was the only other potential claimant, but Heath had a delicate juggling act to perform with his senior colleagues. Having groomed no-one for the Lord Chancellorship, he now elevated Hogg to the Woolsack (re-enobled as Lord Hailsham), leaving Maudling to take the Home Office. Christopher Soames might have been a rival for the Foreign Secretaryship had he not lost his seat in 1966. So Sir Alec returned, almost ten years after his first appointment to the post by Harold Macmillan. Even so, it was widely assumed that he would not stay in office for more than a year or 18 months before making way for a younger man. There was also a curious parallel with the situation which had existed in 1960. Once again the Heath-Home relationship would be crucial to the administration of the country's foreign relations and, though Heath as Prime Minister was now the senior partner, the division of responsibility was remarkably similar. Once again Heath focused on Europe, leaving Douglas-Home to handle most of the rest – East-West relations, Africa and the Middle and Far East. It was not an arrangement which every Foreign Secretary would have found it easy to accept. Douglas-Home had witnessed at close quarters the way in which a Foreign Secretary, over-sensitive about his position (Eden) had bridled at the interference of a domineering Prime Minister (Chamberlain). But, as he had when serving Macmillan, Douglas-Home readily accepted the Premier's definition and delimitation of his powers. The presence as Defence Secretary of Lord Carrington, one of Heath's inner circle, with a wide-ranging brief as a sort of diplomatic trouble-shooter, was a further potential problem which Douglas-Home found no difficulty in accommodating. A mutual confidence between the two men, which went back to Douglas-Home's appointment of Carrington as High Commissioner to Australia in 1956, prevented any serious friction.

Yet if there were elements of *déjà vu* about Douglas-Home's return to the Foreign Office, there had also been significant changes from the position that had existed in 1960. At that time Britain could still claim, with some credibility, to be the world's third-ranking power with influence – sometimes pre-eminent – to shape developments in many regions of the globe. The intervening years had witnessed a rapid decline in the country's relative power and a consequential reduction in its capacity to determine events. Though British leaders would continue trying to punch above the country's weight, the old Churchillian notion of three inter-linking circles – the Atlantic partnership, the Commonwealth and Western Europe – giving Britain a unique capacity to impact upon world affairs, had finally had its day. Heath, with his single-minded European fixation, certainly realised this. But so too did Douglas-Home. The Commonwealth and the Special Relationship were both assets of dwindling importance, though the Foreign Secretary still placed greater weight on keeping in step with the United States than did the Prime Minister, not least because of his continuing consciousness of the Soviet threat.

Douglas-Home's renewed ministerial career did not begin auspiciously. Visiting South Africa in 1968 he had promised Prime Minister Vorster that a future Conservative government would resume the sale of arms in line with the Simonstown Agreement of 1955. Seeing South Africa as a pivotal point in the defence of the South Atlantic, he was concerned by the need to safeguard routes to the east, not least because of the closure of the Suez Canal in 1967. But he seems to have given insufficient consideration to the possible reactions to a change in British policy. The matter came before the first Cabinet meeting of the new government on 23 June. Liberal opinion was outraged and the administration's overseas policy got off to the worst possible start. The reaction of the Commonwealth – Pierre Trudeau in Canada and Mrs Gandhi in India – was particularly shrill. The Foreign Secretary's presentation of his case to the Commons was little short of a disaster, not least as he twice referred to Harold Wilson as the Prime Minister. Douglas Houghton, chairman of the Parliamentary Labour party, judged that he had immediately made himself 'expendable'. A few weeks later he spoke of Tanganyika, instead of Tanzania, only to be met with an audible aside of 'He means German East Africa' from Labour's Michael Stewart. Rumours abounded that he was ill, perhaps that he had suffered a minor stroke. One who had known him a long time suggested that the problem was his age – 'he is a very old sixty-seven'.[15] But Heath, shaken by the sudden death of his Chancellor of the Exchequer, Iain Macleod, on 20 July, was in no mood to face further disruption to the Cabinet. Sir Alec's position was safe.

One of the reasons for his South African policy may have been the hope of securing that country's assistance in effecting a settlement of the Rhodesian problem. It was very much a case of resuming responsibility for an issue that had confronted him during the months of his premiership, for the Wilson years had witnessed much drama but little progress towards a resolution of what was the most serious outstanding legacy of Britain's imperial past. High-profile talks with the Rhodesian premier, Ian Smith, aboard HMS *Tiger* in December 1966 and HMS *Fearless* in October 1968 had produced little beyond mutual recrimination and charges of bad faith. Having kept the Tory right in check during the years of opposition, Douglas-Home was now expected to bring Rhodesia back to legality without 'selling out' the minority white population. 'It was not difficult to detect that [Heath's] government was anxious and, if this word could ever be used about the placid Sir Alec Douglas-Home, was passionately anxious to obtain an agreement.'[16] Indeed, a succession of right-wing British visitors had planted the idea in Salisbury that the Conservative government would accept just about any terms in order to rid itself of the Rhodesian incubus. This was never Douglas-Home's position, but the resumption of arms sales to South Africa did seem to indicate a predisposition to make concessions to the illegal regime.

On 9 November 1971 he announced to the Commons that he would be going to Salisbury to see whether a settlement was possible. It would have to be on the basis of the so-called 'Five Principles' which Douglas-Home himself had laid down before losing office in 1964. Of these the most important was that which called for 'unimpeded progress to majority rule'. This fell some way short of the sixth principle, added by Wilson, which insisted that there could be No Independence Before Majority African Rule (NIBMAR), an addition which Douglas-Home regarded as a *terrible mistake*.[17] Hopes for a settlement were high. Ian Smith at least trusted the British Foreign Secretary and he also enjoyed the confidence of the Conservative right. Much of the groundwork was carried out by the skilled negotiator and lawyer, Lord Goodman. Then, accompanied by Goodman and the Attorney General, Sir Peter Rawlinson, Douglas-Home led ten days of difficult negotiations before reaching a settlement to be put to the Rhodesian people.

The provisional agreement was 'within the Five Principles – if only just within'.[18] Many concessions had been made to the Smith regime. The basis of the future Rhodesian constitution was not to be the colonial one of 1961 nor even that of 1965 following UDI, but the newly proclaimed republican constitution of 1969. Africans could now, in the long run, look forward to holding a majority in the national assembly, but 'the run still seemed likely to be a very long one indeed'.[19] This was in line with the sort of thinking Douglas-Home had displayed as Commonwealth Secretary in the late 1950s. The timescale would allow Africans the time to become educated and prepare for self-government. *I sometimes fear those who advocate the best and will not look at the second best*, he told the Bishop of Edinburgh. *The Africans in Rhodesia have no chance of asserting themselves without a blood-bath, so I must advise them to take it gradually or not at all. I will weep for them if they turn down the chance.*[20] But turn it down they did. The Pearce Commission, charged with determining whether the proposed deal was acceptable to all sections of the Rhodesian population, duly reported that it did not enjoy the support of the black majority. Douglas-Home continued to believe that this outcome reflected more their dislike and distrust of Ian Smith than it did the merits of the provisional agreement itself.

The Africans in Rhodesia have no chance of asserting themselves without a bloodbath, so I must advise them to take it gradually or not at all.

DOUGLAS-HOME

Notwithstanding Britain's diminished and still diminishing stature in world affairs, the on-going Cold War remained at the heart of all foreign policy considerations in the early 1970s. Memories of the Soviet suppression of Czechoslovakia in 1968 were deeply engrained. Douglas-Home remained concerned by evidence of Soviet expansion as shown by the deployment of the Soviet navy in the Mediterranean and east of Suez. For some time he seemed, if anything, even more wary than in the 1960s of moves towards peaceful co-existence between East and West, such as the Ostpolitik pursued by the West German Chancellor, Willy Brandt. Indeed, Anglo-Soviet relations hit a short-term nadir in the autumn of 1971 when the Foreign Secretary decided to reduce the swollen ranks of Soviet diplomatic and consular staff in Britain, many of whom were using their official positions to conceal covert intelligence activity. As many as 105 Soviet 'diplomats' were expelled. Whatever it did for international relations, the move was generally well received in Britain. Douglas-Home's popularity rating went up 16 points, leaving him with the highest rating of any Cabinet minister. Yet within a few months Douglas-Home was advising his colleagues that it was time to adopt a more positive policy towards the Eastern bloc. British exports to communist countries lagged behind those of her European competitors. Slowly, bilateral relations improved and the Foreign Secretary himself made a brief visit to Moscow in December 1973. He was also concerned not to leave the second great communist state, China, out of the equation. He used an address to the United Nations General Assembly, as early as September 1970, at least to speculate that Communist China's admission to that organisation might have a beneficial effect. *Their intentions, in the opinion of the British Government, should be put to the proof here in this Assembly of nations.*[21] In March 1972 it was announced that the two countries would exchange ambassadors, thus ending a period of more than two decades in which interests had been represented by chargés d'affaires. This move necessitated the downgrading of Britain's representation in Taiwan, which was now acknowledged to be part of the Chinese People's Republic. To set the seal on this diplomatic breakthrough, Douglas-Home paid a five-day official visit to Peking in October.

In the meantime Heath pursued and secured his life-long goal of British membership of the European Economic Community. Douglas-Home never matched the Prime Minister's passion for the European cause, but he had long believed that Britain had no real alternative to membership. Though detailed negotiations with the Community were left to Geoffrey Rippon under Heath's overall direction, Douglas-Home did chair the Cabinet's European Policy Committee. Writing in a pamphlet published in June 1971 and entitled *Our European Destiny*, he declared his full agreement on two counts with the most fervent opponent of British membership, Enoch Powell. *The first is that our application is a step of the utmost political significance, and the second is that there is a danger of its being overlooked in the public debate on the economic issues.*[22] But he seems not to have given any deep consideration to the question of lost sovereignty, nor to have speculated on what the process of 'ever closer union' envisaged by the Treaty of Rome might ultimately entail. At the same time he was more concerned than Heath to balance any commitment to Europe with a continuing close relationship with the United States, whose President, Richard Nixon, he somewhat unexpectedly admired.

Overall, Douglas-Home's partnership with Heath worked well. With his domestic administration in some disarray, it suited the Prime Minister to have a respected figure of stature in charge of foreign affairs. Douglas-Home recovered from his uncertain start and was widely regarded as among the more successful members of the Cabinet. There were differences between the Foreign Office and Number 10, as for example over the Indo-Pakistani war of 1971, but nothing to cause an open breach. Perhaps the most dangerous situation arose in the government's last weeks when Douglas-Home preferred an Atlanticist and Heath a European response to the Yom Kippur War and the resulting oil crisis. An incipient rift might have become publicly apparent had the government itself not fallen

> The 37th President of the United States, Richard Nixon (1913–94) was elected in 1968 on a platform of bringing the Vietnam War to an end, but ordered the bombing of Cambodia in 1969. He also pursued better relations with the Soviet Union and especially with Communist China, which, like Douglas-Home, he visited in 1972. That same year he won the largest victory in a US presidential election, with 60 per cent of the popular vote and carrying 49 of the 50 states. Yet the Watergate Scandal brought him down, and he resigned in 1974. His successor Gerald Ford granted him a blanket pardon.

in February 1974. Only occasionally did the Foreign Secretary stray beyond his departmental brief. In 1972 he backed the Home Secretary, Robert Carr, against right-wing opposition in upholding Britain's obligations to expelled Ugandan Asians and in persuading other Commonwealth countries to share Britain's responsibilities. In private he argued unsuccessfully, and somewhat surprisingly, against direct rule for Northern Ireland, believing that Britain's interests would be best served by pushing the people of the province towards the concept of a united Ireland.

There were repeated rumours of his impending retirement or of a possible move to the Scottish Office in an attempt to restore Tory fortunes north of the border. But Douglas-Home was happy where he was – as was his wife – and he had now become 'the one unsackable member of the Cabinet'.[23] Indeed, as Heath's own standing with the public declined, it was, as one observer put it, a case of 'Alec can get rid of Ted but not vice versa'.[24] The Foreign Secretary enjoyed the respect of his officials in the Foreign Office and in large measure the regard of foreign statesmen who admired his clarity of expression and who liked the fact that they knew where they stood with him. But this Indian Summer of Douglas-Home's career was at the mercy of events beyond his control. By the end of 1973 a dispute with the National Union of Mineworkers was threatening the government's very existence. Heath's senior advisers divided into those who favoured an early election and those who counselled caution. The Foreign Secretary was in the latter camp, but the former prevailed. Heath decided on 6/7 February 1974 to call an election for 28 February. His appeal to settle who governed the country lacked conviction, and the situation was not helped by Enoch Powell urging voters to support Labour. The vagaries of the British electoral system produced a result in which no single party would have a majority in the new House of Commons. Labour had more seats than the Conservatives, though the latter had polled more votes. A final attempt by Heath to hold on to power by coming to an agreement with the Liberals broke down over his refusal to promise a reform of the electoral system. After several days of confusion Wilson returned, somewhat unexpectedly, to 10 Downing Street. Alec Douglas-Home's long ministerial career was at an end.

Douglas-Home had decided that the 1970 parliament should be his last. The unexpected crisis of 1973–4 and the sudden holding of a general election, a year earlier than might have been anticipated, forced a change of plan and he once again successfully defended his seat of Kinross and West Perthshire in February 1974. But with the Conservatives' loss of office and the perhaps imminent prospect of another election, he saw that it was time to make his intentions clear and allow the local party to choose a new candidate. In a press statement on 22 March 1974 he let it be known that, at nearly 71, he would not again seek re-election. None the less, Heath reappointed him as Shadow Foreign Secretary and he remained active on the Tory front bench until Parliament was again dissolved in September. During this time he formed a good working relationship with his Labour successor, James Callaghan. The issue of Europe again occupied centre stage. In a clever attempt to maintain at least a semblance of party unity, Harold Wilson agreed to a policy of renegotiating Britain's terms of entry and putting the resulting settlement to national approval via a referendum. Home wanted no part of such a constitutional innovation. *We are in the Community*, he reminded Heath, *and intend to lead in the way we want to go.*[25]

We are in the Community and intend to lead in the way we want to go.

DOUGLAS-HOME

The general election in October hardly clarified the political scene. Labour emerged with a small overall majority of just three seats in the new House of Commons. Douglas-Home now took a life peerage, following the precedent already set by Quintin Hogg, his rival for the leadership in 1963, and resumed his seat in the upper chamber as Baron Home of the Hirsel. But he was too valuable a figure to be allowed to disappear immediately from political prominence. In November, Heath, whose own position was now coming increasingly into question, asked him to chair a committee to reconsider the rules governing elections to the party leadership. There is some evidence that Home sought to ensure that the new arrangements would make it easier to bring about a change, as *the Party will not have Ted.*[26] At all events it was agreed that a successful candidate would now need to have a margin of 15 per cent of all those entitled to vote over his challenger. In 1965 the percentage stipulation had related only to those actually voting. Wags dubbed the new arrangement 'Alec's revenge'. It would one day ensure the downfall of Margaret Thatcher. For all that, Home remained loyal to Heath, but he quickly rallied to Mrs Thatcher once she was elected to succeed him in February 1975. For Home it was very much a case of 'The King is dead. Long live the King' – or in this case, the Queen! With next to no experience of diplomacy and foreign policy, the new leader soon found herself calling upon his accumulated wisdom. Unlucky in her first choice of Shadow Foreign Secretary, the briefly resuscitated Reginald Maudling, who was out of sympathy with the new leader's style and approach and, in any case, now sliding into alcoholism, Mrs Thatcher discovered that Home's strongly held and uncomplicated beliefs chimed well with her own gut instincts, especially on questions relating to the Soviet Union and the Cold War. Later she invited

Home to chair a Conservative committee on the reform of the upper house. Its report, published in March 1978, called for a substantial measure of direct election as the only means of ensuring that the second chamber enjoyed genuine moral authority – a prescription of reform more radical than any yet proposed by the government of Tony Blair.

In October 1976 Home published his memoirs, *The Way the Wind Blows*. Its tone was predictably discreet and self-effacing. It would have been entirely out of character for him to have used this volume to disclose secrets of his ministerial career, to expose the dissensions of Cabinet government or to settle old political scores. A good and easy read, it sold well. It is said that R A Butler would, rather cruelly, offer the book to his house-guests with the characteristically waspish enquiry, 'Would you care to look at this book on fishing?'[27] In some ways *Letters to a Grandson*, published in 1983, was more revealing. Though purportedly written for a teenage audience, it does much to clarify Home's underlying beliefs and convictions.

Margaret Thatcher (b. 1925) became MP for Finchley in the 1959 general election and secured her first government job under Macmillan in 1961. She voted for Edward Heath in the 1964 leadership election and rose to Shadow Cabinet rank by 1967. In the Heath government of 1970–4 she was Education Secretary. She challenged Heath for the leadership in 1975 and won, earning his undying enmity. Winning the 1979 general election, she went on to win two more, making her both the only female and the longest-serving Prime Minister of the 20th century. (See *Thatcher* by Clare Beckett, in this series.)

For some years Home was an assiduous attender in the House of Lords, accompanied for a few years by his old mentor, Harold Macmillan, who enjoyed a brief return to the political twilight as the Earl of Stockton, but Home never used his seniority and status to rock the boat of the Thatcher government. His wife died suddenly in September 1990. Soon afterwards he made his last appearance in Parliament. Before long his own health began to fail. He retreated to the Hirsel where, after several years as a semi-invalid, he died peacefully on 9 October 1995, surrounded by his family.

Chapter 6: Assessment

Asked on the BBC's *Panorama* programme in July 1973, in an interview marking his 70th birthday, what he thought historians would make of his time as Prime Minister, Alec Douglas-Home replied, *Well, I don't think they'll have a chance to give me much of a rating because I was only Prime Minister for just about a year*. This assessment, entirely characteristic of the man who gave it, is one with which it is difficult to quarrel. Douglas-Home's premiership was the shortest of the 20th century with the solitary exception of that of the 'unknown Prime Minister' of the 1920s, Andrew Bonar Law. It came, moreover, as a political suffix, at the end of a long period of Conservative government, its policies largely determined by what had gone before, its agenda by the inevitably imminent general election to come. In so far as he is remembered at all, therefore, it is as a 'kind of tweedy blur on the political landscape ... a Scottish laird with a clipped, aristocratic voice and half-moon glasses'.[1] His brief premiership inevitably forms little more than 'a punctuation mark between the two Harolds [Macmillan and Wilson]' who came before and after him.[2] By his prime ministerial decisions he changed the long-term direction of neither the Conservative Party nor the British state and, with the exception of the ending of Retail Price Maintenance, left few imprints upon his country's legislative history. Notwithstanding the narrow outcome of the

1964 general election, it is no clearer four decades on than it was in 1963 that the Conservatives made the right choice in making him Prime Minister. Strikingly, ten years after the event, Douglas-Home himself discussed the decision to allow his name to go forward into the leadership contest and conceded, *I'm not at all sure to this day that I was right.*[3] Harold Macmillan, his doughtiest supporter at the time, reached a comparable conclusion quicker and with less hesitation. 'Alec did his best – with courage and dignity. But he could not impress himself on Parlt or people enough for a PM, admirable as he was as ... Foreign Sec.' More basically, Douglas-Home 'didn't have enough fire in his belly – he wouldn't say bugger off ...'.[4]

Had a letter from your father today about inflation ... or deflation, or something.
DOUGLAS-HOME

Would a longer premiership have led to a different conclusion? 'He might well', suggests Reginald Maudling, the man who served him as Chancellor of the Exchequer, 'have become a great Prime Minister if there had been time.'[5] This seems unlikely. While a few extra votes combined with the vagaries of the British electoral system could easily have produced a narrow Conservative victory in 1964, it seems doubtful, granted the rising tide of economic problems, whether a serious defeat could have been avoided soon thereafter. Moreover, history suggests that those Prime Ministers who aspire to greatness take up their positions with a clear vision of the direction in which they wish to lead the country. In the context of the mid-1960s that vision would have had to relate to Britain's economic performance and it is questionable whether Douglas-Home had either the interest or the expertise to make his mark in this respect. *Had a letter from your father today*, he once wrote with disarming frankness to the journalist Dominic Harrod, *about inflation ... or deflation, or something.*[6] With his celebrated reliance on matchsticks, there was something about him which appealed to the British admiration for the self-confessed amateur. But in the hard political reality of the time his near-illiteracy in economics was a considerable handicap. As he later admitted, *I was not familiar with economics. They had never come my way. Nor have I been encouraged ever since to think there's an exact science. But it was a weakness. If I had thought I was going to be Prime Minister, I would have taken more trouble to understand the various theories.*[7]

In any case, whatever the length of his premiership had been, Douglas-Home was not the sort of man who would have tried to impose a clearly thought-out set of ideas on to his party, still less his country. It is not possible, in fact, to envisage anything in the nature of 'Homeism'. He was not an original thinker, his mind not given to intellectual curiosity. His commonsensical and practical approach to politics and to problem solving left little room for speculative flights of fancy. Strikingly, when, soon after his appointment as Prime Minister, it was proposed that an anthology of his statements on domestic policy might be published to bring him to the attention of a wider public, the Conservative Research Department opposed the idea, not least because the quotations involved were 'not very impressive'.[8] As has been seen, his basic attitudes were often to the right of those of the majority of his Conservative contemporaries. He cited with approval the dictum of Abraham Lincoln that the poor are not made richer by making the rich poorer and he was ready to defend selection in education on the grounds that a comprehensive system was likely to move at the pace of the slowest pupil. But his ideas were largely unexceptionable and scarcely added up to a coherent ideology.

Sir Alec, suggested an early biographer, 'was neither a Burke nor a Coleridge. His cast of mind was religious, not philosophical, intuitive, practical, a man of principle rather than principles'.[9] His Christian commitment, uncomplicated but profound, was at the heart of his entire life. *In short, I concluded that the complex ordering of nature which included man could not be the work of chance.* But he had no time for the doctrinal subtleties of theological dispute. *I was, and am, impatient of the muddle and confusion and division which the Churches have made of the simple message of Christ, but then man has a habit of creating his own troubles.*[10] He admitted the influence of his old headmaster (and later father-in-law) Dr Alington, who became Dean of Durham Cathedral, on his religious thinking and also, rather surprisingly, that of the American evangelist, Billy Graham. *I cannot say that I was particularly attracted by the spectacular stage-management of his Christian circus, but he got results.*[11] Such religious convictions rather than any political ideology determined the course of his career in public life. 'He had a Christian sense of right and wrong,' recalled his Foreign Office private secretary, 'and then what was right for his country. And he believed in democracy and free enterprise and hated Communism and totalitarianism and oppression. Then, of course, much lower down the scale – didn't really feature very much! – what was right for the Conservative Party.'[12]

The path to the British premiership is strewn with pitfalls and all those who succeed in reaching their destination need a fair measure of luck to accompany them. This was certainly the case with Alec Douglas-Home. Without the coincidence of Macmillan's sudden indisposition and the government's bill to allow peers to disclaim their titles, his candidature might never have got off the ground. If the succession crisis had come three months earlier or nine months later, it would have required additional enabling legislation for him to return to the House of Commons. But he was also unlucky in the time and circumstances in which he entered 10 Downing Street. Not only did he take over when the electorate was becoming disenchanted with a long-serving and now accident-prone Tory government and when the politics of the post-war Keynesian consensus seemed no longer capable of providing all the answers to the problems of the British economy. He also found himself opposed, in Harold Wilson, by a newly-installed opposition leader who had quickly captured the popular imagination. For a time, Wilson's style 'seemed to change the national psyche and with it the electoral landscape'.[13] The contest between the two men seemed no contest at all, 'lower middle-class against aristocratic, innovator against traditionalist, statistician against self-avowed innumerate, golfer against keen shot and fisherman, technocrat against territorial magnate, Montagu Burton against Savile Row or scruffy tweeds, professional against amateur, the future against the past'.[14] In all the circumstances it can only be wondered at that Douglas-Home emerged from this unequal confrontation as well as he did. Wilson's moment did not last. Within a few years the Labour leader's image had transmogrified into that of an over-clever political salesman, his product shoddy and his trust devalued even if, as he claimed, the pound in his pocket had not been. But it was Douglas-Home's misfortune that his own brief ascendancy found Wilson at the height of his powers and prestige.

More generally, Sir Alec also took over at a time when his own very real qualities were at a discount. In the early 1960s British society moved, quite rapidly, from the still deferential class structure of the post-war era to a new age dominated by a questioning and irreverent younger generation, by Carnaby Street and the Beatles. Douglas-Home was an inherently unlikely figure to ride out this cultural transformation. It was a new experience for many to hear a present or recent Prime Minister of Great Britain being described by Richard Ingrams and Bernard Levin respectively as a 'half-witted Earl who looked and behaved like something out of P G Wodehouse' or simply as a 'cretin'.[15] The Conservative Party had moved from a Prime Minister frequently pictured on the grouse moor to one who actually owned his own. Small wonder that Wilson could not believe his luck. 'Had I seen yesterday's newspapers?' the Labour leader asked an American journalist, 'showing Home with a sticking plaster on his jaw, accompanying a group of cronies on a shoot. "We could not find the money to pay for better election propaganda. The Tories insist on continuing an image completely remote from the ordinary people and the youth of Britain."'[16] Nor were such sentiments confined to Labour's ranks. Learning of the possibility of Douglas-Home's selection, the junior minister Reginald Bevins warned of the probable dire electoral consequences. 'The most important man in my constituency is my agent, and he insists that we couldn't expect to hold a single seat in Liverpool if a fourteenth Earl were chosen. It'd be electoral suicide for us – they must know that.'[17] Bevin's forecast was unduly gloomy. But four of the six Tory seats in this once Conservative stronghold did fall to Labour a year later.

The element of luck in Douglas-Home's ascent of Disraeli's greasy pole should not lead to the conclusion that he was a completely accidental Prime Minister. He was, in retirement, inclined to present himself as the most reluctant premier of the 20th century. But Ian Gilmour's wise words merit attention. 'As a rule', he stresses, 'it is safer to judge a man's character by his actions than to judge his actions by what is assumed to be his character.'[18] The account presented above has suggested that his role in the leadership crisis of 1963 was far from passive. Once he had decided that he wanted the job, he moved with speed and determination to outwit his rivals, aided always by the support of the out-going premier Harold Macmillan. The latter vigorously denied that his own role had been 'to influence the choice of my successor. My sole object was to inform the Queen of the results of the investigations which I had made in the Cabinet, among MPs, among Conservative Peers and within the Party organisation.'[19] Yet it is difficult to escape the conclusion that the retiring Prime Minister was driven by a determination that Butler should not succeed him and that, after a brief flirtation with Hailsham, he judged that Douglas-Home was the man best equipped to help him secure this objective. In the latter Macmillan found not a reluctant victim but a willing collaborator. Douglas-Home was 'not ambitious in the sense of wanting to scheme for power, although not foolish enough to resist honour when it comes to him'.[20] He managed to create a contrary impression because of his distinctive and somewhat deceptive character. 'It was strong without many of the normal outer signs of strength, decisive without the usual trappings of decisive-

'Iron painted to look like wood.'

MACMILLAN ON DOUGLAS-HOME

ness. Sir Alec was not arrogant, bullying, abrupt, ruthless, cold, egocentric or determinedly charismatic; he did not parade himself as a great orator. On the contrary, he was amiable ... approachable and unfailingly courteous, whether to opponents or to the least important of his party's supporters.'[21] Macmillan once made the same point more succinctly – he was 'iron painted to look like wood'.[22]

Whatever his faults and failings, Douglas-Home was, over the course of a parliamentary career that encompassed more than four decades, a thoroughly professional politician, and one who enjoyed the exercise of power, or at least *participation at the centre of things.*[23] The supposedly reluctant Prime Minister was soon confessing that he liked his new job. *Naturally, at first there were some strange aspects and I had to do things I was unused to, such as appointing bishops. And I had to get the feel of the House of Commons again ... But I do feel that I can handle it and that it isn't too much of a strain. You have to organize yourself and your time. I find I can manage this.*[24] And it is worth noting that no post-war Foreign Secretary served in that position at a more advanced age than he did. One observer found him, shortly before his 70th birthday, 'enjoying himself enormously at the Foreign Office ... and he shows no sign at all of retiring. He takes a very short view of politics in general, delegates awkward subjects ... to others ... and goes on his way swanning around the world on goodwill missions.'[25]

In recognising the importance of ambition in Douglas-Home's political make-up, it is not necessary to deny the presence also of a very genuine sense of pubic service. Such a concept was instilled into him at an early age. *My father*, he recalled, *used to din into my head week in and week out that the purpose of life was to give service to other people.*[26] He repeated the same sentiment when asked, in the early weeks of his premiership, to set down a statement of his political philosophy. *I went into politics*, he then insisted, *because I felt that it was a form of public service and that as nearly a generation of politicians had been cut down in the first war, those who had anything to give in the way of leadership ought to do so.*[27] It was his misfortune, however, that Douglas-Home came to the forefront of political life, when, in a climate of cynicism and satire, it was too easy to dismiss such expressions of social obligation as facile or insincere. But his career lasted long enough for that mood to pass. By the end of the 1960s, still more after the setbacks and disappointments of the 1970s, it was

Douglas-Home's Premiership

'Alec Home ... could well lay claim to being, in terms of personal organisation, the most effective post-war premier since Attlee at combating personal overload in the lack of fuss with which he dispatched his paperwork and his exhortations to colleagues to curb the wordiness of their submissions. It is no coincidence that Home and Attlee were the least media-conscious of the occupants of No. 10 since 1945. For both of them cricket reports ranked above the political columns in the scale of newspaper importance and they got on very well personally. Harold Wilson thought Home "was idle". I think he was sensible and, unlike Wilson, Alec Home did not confuse "work-rate" with effectiveness. And in his quiet way, he was an efficient dispatcher of business (Douglas Hurd noticed his "great gift for absorbing the essentials out of things – he only wrote four or five words often, a couple of sentences at the top in that spidery red hand, but the thing ran well"). Home did not believe in overwork. He would take time out for the pleasures of the vase. He is, without question, the most famous flower-arranger in British political history and there is a charming picture of him at work on the tulips and the daffodils on the back cover of Kenneth Young's 1970 biography. He was careful with food and drink and developed the interesting habit of taking his meals at London times wherever he was in the world.'

Alec Douglas-Home really was the first thoroughbred countryman in Downing Street since Stanley Baldwin. Yet there was a moderniser lurking beneath the hacking jacket. As he wrote in his memoirs, *The Way the Wind Blows*: ... "I confess that I would like to have been given a bit longer at No. 10 so as to get more grip on the machinery of government. The keys to this are: short and precise paper-work; a chain of government committees each charged to take decisions, resulting in a Cabinet agenda which is cleared of all but the absolute essentials; Ministers who can be relied upon to insist on these rules ...; and lastly a programme of legislation for Parliament which is not overloaded."' [Hennessy, *The Prime Minister*, pp 282–3.]

once again acceptable for a politician to be a 'gent' or even a 'toff'. From an even longer-term perspective, in an age of soundbites, spin and voter apathy, and with politicians of all parties now enjoying a lower standing in public esteem than at any time in the entire 20th century, he stands out as a man of unimpeachable integrity, a beacon of political rectitude. 'He faced a challenge as daunting as has ever confronted a new leader', judged one veteran of British politics, 'and he went about it with honesty, sincerity and integrity, without gimmicks, flamboyance or theatrical props.'[28] This was essentially true at the time; but it seems an even more appropriate assessment four decades on.

Rather than his politics or his ideas, therefore, it is perhaps Douglas-Home's personal qualities which have left the most indelible mark. His brother William was well placed to describe his character. 'I would say one sensed in him a kind of calmness such as one feels in the atmosphere around a mountain loch – a shade forbidding, perhaps, to a stranger … but, to all its familiars a well-loved landmark, comforting, impressive and serene.'[29] His prime-ministerial memorial lies more in the impression which he made on those with whom he worked than in any legislative or ideological legacy. Enoch Powell, a man not given to praise for the sake of form alone and who, of course, refused to serve in his government, nonetheless 'regarded Alec as the rarest thing in politics – a politician whose word one could trust'.[30] According to Peter Carrington, 'he aroused considerable loyalty and where there is strong loyalty to a Premier within Cabinet that loyalty spreads laterally and members find it more natural to support each other'.[31] James Margach, whose long journalistic career brought him into contact with all British Prime Ministers from Ramsay MacDonald to James Callaghan, had no hesitation in concluding that, in terms of the standards of conduct which he set for himself and others, 'he excelled all the Prime Ministers I know'.[32] In a similarly generous tribute Douglas Hurd ranked him alongside King Hussein of Jordan and Nelson Mandela as the politest man with whom he had ever dealt. For Peter Rawlinson, who served alongside him as a law officer in the Conservative governments of the 1960s and 1970s, Douglas-Home was the only man he ever encountered in public life 'without a spark of vanity or pretension or that streak of unpleasantness which seems essential for those who reach the top of Dizzy's greasy pole'.[33] But, for all these commendable qualities, there remained sections of mankind with whose patterns of thought the privileged, aristocratic Douglas-Home found it difficult to empathise, be they the aspiring populations of colonial Africa or the unemployed workers of his Lanark constituency. Writing in 1964, an early and unsympathetic biographer reminded his readers that, during the Depression of the 1930s, the then Lord Dunglass had suggested to the Commons that unemployed coal miners and their families could be transported from Scotland to the Home Counties to work as domestic servants.

For all the qualifications that have been made, the year-long Douglas-Home premiership is not without its historical importance — almost despite the Prime Minister himself. With hindsight it can be seen to occupy a crucial position in the development of the modern Conservative Party and, more generally, of the British state itself. The manner in which he was selected, in what Ben Pimlott has described as 'the most confused and unsatisfactory transfer of office of the post-war period',[34] permanently discredited the so-called 'customary processes' and ensured that they could never again be used to choose either the Prime Minister of Great Britain or the leader of the Tory Party. Throughout his time in Downing Street, and even subsequently as Leader of the Opposition,

Douglas-Home never fully overcame the accusation that his appointment had resulted from the machinations of a self-serving 'magic circle' of Conservative grandees. It was thus the least 'democratic' Prime Minister of modern times, an hereditary peer without to begin with even a seat in the House of Commons, who finally drove the Tories to adopt the processes of democracy. Under his guidance the party instituted a formal and open method of electing the party leader. This change had a profound impact upon the type of men – and the woman – who followed him in the Conservative leadership. The 14th Earl was succeeded by the son of a carpenter and a lady's maid, a grocer's daughter from Grantham and the son of a trapeze artist who went to neither public school nor university. It is difficult to envisage the 'customary processes' producing any of these outcomes. At the same time the events of 1963 effectively destroyed the royal prerogative, notwithstanding Macmillan's insistent protestations that he acted above all to preserve it. In all but the most exceptional of circumstances, the choice of the Crown's first minister has now been removed from the monarch of the day.

Douglas-Home's perceived weaknesses have profoundly affected the subsequent evolution of Britain's electoral politics. No where is this more the case than in relation to the Prime Minister's media image. Churchill had despised television; Eden, in his wilder moments, concluded that the BBC was a hotbed of left-wing dissidents. But the fact remained that, by the mid-1960s, it had become essential for political leaders to be competent performers on the small screen. Even before the 1964 election Douglas-Home was traumatised by the whole experience of appearing before a mass audience sitting in their living rooms. He recalled an encounter with a make-up girl.

Can you not make me look better than I do on television? I
look rather scraggy, like a ghost.
  'No'
  Why not?
  'Because you have a head like a skull.'
  Does not everyone have a head like a skull?
  'No'.[35]

Likewise, Douglas-Home's fateful appearance in Birmingham's Rag Market now stands as a seminal moment in the long-term transition from the open hustings of the Victorian era to the carefully orchestrated, ticket-only election rallies of the modern era. That his submission to hecklers was transmitted to a mass television audience compounded the damage a hundredfold. *It produced an appearance of strain which inevitably conveyed itself to the television onlookers – I looked rather hunted and that had a bad effect. I blame myself for not studying the techniques of television more than I did.*[36] After 1964 electoral strategists in all parties understood that the appearance of their leaders could actually determine the voters' verdict. Peter Hennessy puts the point with brutal clarity – 'no more aristocrats, skulls or half-moon glasses'.[37]

In the evolution of the post-war Conservative Party the two years of Douglas-Home's leadership clearly marked a turning-point. Until the end of the 1964 government the Tories had located themselves ever more firmly in the centre ground of British politics. Critics of the new right would later claim that they had adapted far too readily to the agenda of the Attlee government's post-war settlement with the result that Conservatives had become more interventionist and welfarist than ever before. The party's manifesto for 1959 promised 'to double the standard of living in this generation and to ensure that all sections of society share in the expansion of wealth'. By the early 1960s Conservatives were competing with Labour in the creation and distribution of wealth. This involved ever greater state direction. Such attempts to plan the economy had once been the preserve of the Labour Party. Now it was the Tories who took the lead. Whatever his gut instincts, Douglas-Home as Prime Minister went along with this trend. He had neither the time nor the opportunity to do otherwise. As a result, one commentator has judged that the manifestos of the two leading parties in 1964 were closer together on the central issue of economic policy than at any time in the previous 40 years.[38]

After the 1964 defeat, and partly in response to it, the emphasis began, however tentatively, to change. After all, to persist with policies virtually indistinguishable from Labour's only made sense if the electorate continued to vote Conservative. Once in opposition the Tories had little option but to move to the right if the voters were going to be offered an alternative to the new Labour government. Douglas-Home's key decision was to appoint Edward Heath to head a wide-ranging policy review. The resulting document, *Putting Britain Right Ahead*, published in October 1965 three months after Douglas-Home had given up the leadership, revealed the change. With little mention of the National Economic Development Council or of incomes policies, it stressed ideas of competition and incentives, a shift from direct to indirect taxation and greater selectivity in the provision of social services, all of which seemed to indicate a conscious break with the past. By the time of the Conservatives' manifesto for the 1966 general election, the change was even more apparent. *Action not Words* spoke of reducing income tax, offering greater incentives to managers, breaking up monopolies and increasing competition.

Douglas-Home's own role in this transformation should

not be overstated. It was more a case of the chronological coincidence of the man and the moment. Notwithstanding his own, sometimes private, views, his tendency in government was to veer towards the centre ground. He was by instinct a consensual politician. *I conclude ... that the party leaders should exercise that restraint in the use of the power of the majority to a point where it is not necessary for an Opposition to pledge itself to undo what the government of the day has done.*[39] Furthermore, the rightward reorientation of the Conservative Party under Edward Heath was never ideologically based. For Heath it was all a question of efficiency, preparing Britain to face the bracing competition of the European Community; and Heath himself found it necessary to retreat once more to the centre ground of British politics after the failure in government of many of the policies upon which he was elected in 1970. Not until the arrival of Margaret Thatcher as party leader in 1975 did Conservative politics start to become firmly anchored in a right-of-centre ideology. For all that, in the context of 60 years in the history of the Tory party, the leadership of Alec Douglas-Home still appears to mark the end of one era and the tentative beginning of another.

Like Anthony Eden, under whom he first achieved Cabinet rank, Douglas-Home deserves to be judged on the basis of his whole career rather than upon a brief period as Prime Minister. Like Eden, too, he was most at home in, and left his most lasting mark upon, the realm of foreign affairs. He should, thought Macmillan, be compared with Edward Grey rather than with Herbert Asquith. Over his two spells at the Foreign Office Douglas-Home was in charge of his country's foreign relations for a total of almost seven years, a longer period than any other holder of the office in the 20th century apart from Grey and Eden. But the Foreign Office is a department where the parameters of potential ministerial achievement are determined as much by the country's strength as by the actions of the individual office holder. Douglas-Home's two spells encompassed a difficult period of transition in which a declining world power moved tentatively towards a new and more limited role in the international arena. By the time of his final retirement in 1974 it seemed that this role had been found following Britain's entry into the EEC a year earlier, although the next three decades would repeatedly show that the country and its leaders had still to be reconciled to a post-imperial identity. Douglas-Home's function was, therefore, to manage the process of retreat, a task which in military terms the Duke of Wellington once judged to be the most difficult test of a general's skill. If this offered limited scope for 'greatness', his performance was certainly better than competent.

Douglas-Home felt as much at home in the world of diplomacy as he was ill at ease in that of economics. It pleased him that foreign affairs were less prone to the ritual of inter-party dispute than were domestic politics. That said, they also afforded him the opportunity to display a level of passion that he seldom displayed in relation to domestic issues. The American Secretary of State, Dean Rusk, recalled him giving Andrei Gromyko 'unshirted hell' for trying to interfere with radar in the western air corridors around Berlin. 'Although he kept his poker face, I think even Gromyko was startled by the intensity of Douglas-Home's words.' Appropriately admonished, the Soviets immediately desisted.[40] Both his periods of office were set against the back-drop of the Cold War and it is easy to dismiss Douglas-Home as a simple cold warrior. He detested communism and all it represented and had no doubts as to the moral superiority of the Anglo-American position in the conflict between East and West. But he was always ready to pursue the paths of diplomacy even if, as a veteran of Munich, he was convinced that successful negotiations can only be conducted from a position of strength. He played, for example, in talks with Dean Rusk, an important role in the early diplomacy which preceded the Partial Test Ban Treaty of 1963. His personal negotiating style was not unlike that of Anthony Eden – firm and patient, but with a fixity of purpose and resolve that was effectively softened by impeccable good manners. (But, unlike Eden, his juniors and subordinates were never subjected to a sudden outburst of temper or petulance.) He knew when not to give way. 'Alec Douglas-Home and I decided', recalled Rusk, 'that we could talk just as long and just as repetitively as Gromyko'[41] – no small achievement in itself. 'He never made a position worse', judged one who worked closely with him, 'and he often made it better.'[42]

Douglas-Home recognised the decline in Britain's power which seriously circumscribed his scope for independent diplomatic initiatives. But he remained convinced that Britain could still play a significant role in world affairs, leading the nations of Western Europe into partnership with the United States. He explained his goal shortly before his return to the Foreign Office in 1970. *I think that the evolution we ought to go for is to be a partner in Europe, but with the knowledge from the start that the European community ought to merge later with an Atlantic community.*[43] This was, perhaps, a case of having his diplomatic cake and eating it. Such a vision had been explicitly rejected by de Gaulle in 1963 in his veto of Britain's first application for membership of the EEC. Britain, the General believed, had to choose between Europe and America. Arguably, however, it has remained at the heart of the country's foreign policy objectives over the 30 and more years since Douglas-Home left the front-line of British politics, the proof for many of Britain's still schizophrenic attitude towards its European identity.

How, then, should Douglas-Home be judged? Margaret Thatcher once suggested that he was the wisest man she had ever met. Such praise seems excessive, but his wisdom perhaps lay in keeping his political life in perspective. The pursuit of power never obsessed him. If he was by no stretch of the imagination a great Prime Minister, he had at least the satisfaction of knowing that he left each of the political offices he held having performed better in it than had been widely expected. Even as Prime Minister he almost snatched victory from the jaws of defeat in the general election of 1964. His was at least one of the most contented political retirements of the 20th century, with few feelings of regret about tasks left undone and peaks still to climb. Alec Douglas-Home's worthy career stands perhaps as a honourable exception to Enoch Powell's well known dictum that all political careers, except those truncated in mid-stream by the hand of fate, are bound to end in failure.

NOTES

Chapter 1: Early Life and Career (1903–55)

1. K Young, *Sir Alec Douglas-Home* (Dent, London: 1970) p 3.
2. Lord Home, *The Way the Wind Blows* (Collins, London: 1976) p 14, hereafter *Wind Blows*.
3. *Wind Blows*, p 22.
4. *Wisden* cited in J Ramsden, *The Winds of Change: Macmillan to Heath, 1957–1975* (Longman, London: 1996) p 215.
5. C Connolly, *Enemies of Promise* (Penguin, Harmondsworth: 1961) p 294.
6. Young, *Douglas-Home*, p 23.
7. Young, *Douglas-Home*, p 26.
8. N Skelton, *Constructive Conservatism* (Blackwood, Edinburgh: 1924) p 9.
9. Young, *Douglas-Home*, p 39.
10. Young, *Douglas-Home*, p 46.
11. Young, *Douglas-Home*, p 41.
12. R R James (ed), *Chips: Diaries of Sir Henry Channon* (Weidenfeld and Nicolson, London: 1967) p 198
13. Lord Home, *Letters to a Grandson* (Collins, London: 1983) p 51, hereafter *Letters to Grandson*.
14. *Wind Blows*, p 65.
15. *Wind Blows*, p 66.
16. J Colville, *The Fringes of Power: Downing Street Diaries 1939–1955* (Hodder and Stoughton, London: 1985) p 57, hereafter Colville, *Fringes*.
17. Colville, *Fringes*, p 122.

18. *Wind Blows*, p 88.
19. S Ball (ed), *Parliament and Politics in the Age of Churchill and Attlee: the Headlam Diaries 1935–1951* (Cambridge University Press, London: 1999) p 320.
20. House of Commons Debates, 5th Series, vol 403, col 519.
21. Ball (ed), *Parliament and Politics*, p 422.
22. N Nicolson (ed), *Harold Nicolson: Diaries and Letters 1939–45* (Collins, London: 1967) p 436.
23. Young, *Douglas-Home*, p 68.
24. *The Times*, 12 March 1946.
25. J Dickie, *The Uncommon Commoner: a Study of Sir Alec Douglas-Home* (Pall Mall Press, London: 1964) p 86.
26. A Howard and R West, *The Making of the Prime Minister* (Cape, London: 1965) p 93, hereafter Howard and West, *Making*.
27. *Wind Blows*, p 103.

Chapter 2: Cabinet Minister (1955–63)

1. J Stuart, *Within the Fringe* (Bodley Head, London: 1967) p 162.
2. P Catterall (ed), *The Macmillan Diaries: the Cabinet Years 1950–1957* (Macmillan, London: 2003) pp 593–4.
3. Young, *Douglas-Home*, p 87; R Lamb, *The Failure of the Eden Government* (Sidgwick and Jackson, London: 1987) pp 13–14, hereafter Lamb, *Failure*.
4. P Hennessy, *Muddling Through: Power, Politics and the Quality of Government in Postwar Britain* (Indigo, London: 1997) p 145.
5. D R Thorpe, *Selwyn Lloyd* (Cape, London: 1989) p 265.
6. Young, *Douglas-Home*, p 91.
7. National Archives, PREM 11/1152, Home to Eden 24 Aug 1956.

8. PREM 11/1152, Home to Eden 24 Aug 1956.

9. W Clark, *From Three Worlds* (Sidgwick and Jackson, London: 1986) p 178.

10. Lamb, *Failure*, p 250.

11. Hennessy, *Muddling Through*, p 239.

12. Colville, *Fringes,* p 722.

13. Young, *Douglas-Home*, p 108.

14. R Shepherd, *Iain Macleod* (Hutchinson, London: 1994) p 197.

15. A Horne, *Macmillan 1957–1986* (Macmillan, London: 1989) p 201.

16. H Macmillan, *Riding the Storm 1956–1959* (Macmillan, London: 1971) p 702.

17. Ramsden, *Winds of Change*, p 23.

18. Young, *Douglas-Home*, pp 102, 105.

19. Lamb, *Failure*, pp 21–2.

20. H Macmillan, *Pointing the Way 1959–1961* (Macmillan, London: 1972) p 230.

21. W S Churchill, *His Father's Son: the Life of Randolph Churchill* (Weidenfeld and Nicolson, London: 1996) p 402.

22. Dickie, *Commoner*, p 126

23. Ramsden, *Winds of Change*, p 131.

24. *Wind Blows*, p 157.

25. *Wind Blows*, p 148.

26. *Wind Blows*, p 171.

27. *Letters to Grandson*, p 109.

28. *Wind Blows*, p 154.

29. C L Sulzberger, *The Last of the Giants* (Weidenfeld and Nicolson, London: 1972) p 686.

30. A Gromyko, *Memoirs* (Hutchinson, London: 1989) p 158.

31. Young, *Douglas-Home*, p 138.

32. Sulzberger, *Giants*, p 897.

33. R Lamb, *The Macmillan Years 1957–1963: the Emerging Truth* (John Murray, London: 1995) p 227.

34. D R Thorpe, *Alec Douglas-Home* (Sinclair-Stevenson, London: 1996) p 18.

35. Thorpe, *Douglas-Home*, p 240.

36. *The Times* 26 June 1961.

37. J Morgan (ed), *The Backbench Diaries of Richard Crossman* (Hamish Hamilton, London: 1981) p 1004.

38. Young, *Douglas-Home*, p 143.

Chapter 3: The Succession (1963)

1. J Margach, *The Anatomy of Power* (W H Allen, London: 1981) p 7.

2. Ramsden, *Winds of Change*, p 201.

3. Horne, *Macmillan 1957–1986*, p 532.

4. P Goodhart, *The 1922: the Story of the 1922 Committee* (Macmillan, London: 1973) p 191.

5. Horne, *Macmillan 1957–1986*, p 533.

6. Horne, *Macmillan 1957–1986*, p 536.

7. R S Churchill, *The Fight for the Tory Leadership: a Contemporary Chronicle* (Heinemann, London: 1964) p 103.

8. Lord Hailsham, *A Sparrow's Flight* (Collins, London: 1990) p 352.

9. H Evans, *Downing Street Diary: The Macmillan Years 1957–1963* (Hodder, London: 1981) p 299.

10. Horne, *Macmillan 1957–1986*, p 553.

11. G Lewis, *Lord Hailsham* (Cape, London: 1997) pp 229–30.

12. H Macmillan, *At the End of the Day 1961–1963* (Macmillan, London: 1973) p 510.

13. J Boyd-Carpenter, *Way of Life* (Sidgwick and Jackson, London: 1980) pp 175–6.

14. Thorpe, *Douglas-Home*, p 303.

15. R Bevins, *The Greasy Pole: a Personal Account of the Realities of British Politics* (Hodder and Stoughton, London: 1965) p 143.

16. J Prior, *A Balance of Power* (Hamish Hamilton, London: 1986) p 33.

17. I Gilmour and M Garnett, *Whatever Happened to the Tories: the Conservative Party since 1945* (Fourth Estate, London: 1997) p 198.

18. B Pimlott, *The Queen: a biography of Elizabeth II* (Harper Collins, London: 1997) p 330.

19. Pimlott, *Queen*, p 335.

20. Shepherd, *Macleod*, p 332.

21. Macmillan, *End of the Day*, p 515.

22. Pimlott, *Queen*, p 334.

23. S Heffer, *Like the Roman: the Life of Enoch Powell* (Weidenfeld and Nicolson, London: 1998) p 330.

24. A Sampson, *Macmillan: a Study in Ambiguity* (Penguin, Harmondsworth: 1968) p 126.

25. R Shepherd, *Enoch Powell* (Hutchinson, London: 1996) p 244.

Chapter 4: Prime Minister (19 October 1963–16 October 1964)

1. D McKie and C Cook (eds), *The Decade of Disillusion: British Politics in the Sixties* (Macmillan, London: 1972) p 24.

2. T Benn, *Out of the Wilderness: Diaries 1963–67* (Hutchinson, London: 1987) p 70.

3. K Jefferys, *Retreat from New Jerusalem: British Politics 1951–64* (Macmillan, Houndmills: 1997) p 184.

4. Thorpe, *Douglas-Home*, pp 320–1.

5. Benn, *Out of the Wilderness*, p 95.

6. Thorpe, *Douglas-Home*, p 336.

7. Ramsden, *Winds of Change*, p 216.

8. Howard and West, *Making*, p 116.

9. D Butler and A King, *The British General Election of 1964* (Macmillan, London: 1965) p 84.

10. Ramsden, *Winds of Change*, p 215.

11. Young, *Douglas-Home*, p 175.

12. G Hutchinson, *The Last Edwardian at No 10: an Impression of Harold Macmillan* (Quartet, London: 1980) p 141.

13. P Hennessy, *The Prime Minister: the Office and its Holders since 1945* (Penguin, London: 2001) p 280.

14. *Wind Blows*, p 187.

15. E Heath, *The Course of my Life* (Hodder and Stoughton, London: 1998) p 260.

16. Boyd-Carpenter, *Way of Life*, p 183.

17. Thorpe, *Douglas-Home*, p 257.

18. R Maudling, *Memoirs* (Sidgwick and Jackson, London: 1978) p 130.

19. A Denham and M Garnett, *Keith Joseph* (Acumen, Chesham: 2001) p 123.

20. J Ramsden, *The Making of Conservative Party Policy: the Conservative Research Department since 1929* (Longman, London: 1980) p 225.

21. M Cockerell, *Live From Number 10: the Inside Story of Prime Ministers and Television* (Faber and Faber, London: 1989) p 105.

22. Thorpe, *Douglas-Home*, p 366.

23. Howard and West, *Making*, p 219.

24. Young, *Douglas-Home*, p 210.

25. Howard and West, *Making*, pp 187–8.

26. L Baston, *Reggie: the Life of Reginald Maudling* (Sutton, Stroud: 2004) p 233.
27. Young, *Douglas-Home*, p 214.
28. Young, *Douglas-Home*, pp 218–9.

Chapter 5: After Number 10 (1964–95)
1. H Wilson, *The Labour Government 1964–1970: a Personal Record* (Weidenfeld and Nicolson, London: 1971) p 28.
2. R Crossman, *The Diaries of a Cabinet Minister: Minister of Housing 1964–66* (Hamish Hamilton, London: 1975) p 118.
3. *The Times*, 11 January 1965.
4. Heffer, *Enoch Powell*, p 376.
5. Young, *Douglas-Home*, p 226.
6. Thorpe, *Selwyn Lloyd*, p 392.
7. Crossman, *Diaries 1964–66*, p 234.
8. Boyd-Carpenter, *Way of Life*, p 190.
9. Nigel Lawson quoted in Hennessy, *Muddling Through*, p 243.
10. Young, *Douglas-Home*, p 233.
11. S Ball and A Seldon (eds), *Recovering Power: The Conservatives in Opposition since 1867* (Palgrave, Houndmills: 2005) p 195.
12. Young, *Douglas-Home*, p 237.
13. Ramsden, *Winds of Change*, p 296.
14. Ramsden, *Winds of Change*, p 299.
15. C King, *The Cecil King Diary 1970–1974* (Cape, London: 1975) p 47.
16. A Goodman, *Tell Them I'm On My Way* (Chapmans, London: 1993) p 224.
17. Young, *Douglas-Home*, p 246.

18. R Blake, *A History of Rhodesia* (Eyre Methuen, London: 1977) p 404.
19. Blake, *Rhodesia*, p 403.
20. Thorpe, *Douglas-Home*, pp 427–8.
21. F S Northedge, *Descent from Power: British Foreign Policy 1945–1973* (Allen and Unwin, London: 1974) p 311.
22. Gilmour and Garnett, *Whatever Happened*, p 265.
23. King, *Diaries 1970–74*, p 275.
24. King, *Diaries 1970–74*, p 280.
25. Thorpe, *Douglas-Home*, p 443.
26. Ball and Seldon (eds), *Recovering Power,* p 222.
27. Thorpe, *Douglas-Home*, p 453.

Chapter 6: Assessment

1. Hennessy, *Muddling Through*, p 235.
2. Hennessy, *Prime Minister*, p 546.
3. *Panorama*, 2 July 1973.
4. Horne, *Macmillan 1957–1986*, p 582.
5. Maudling, *Memoirs*, p 130.
6. Hennessy, *Prime Minister*, p 273.
7. P Hennessy, *Cabinet* (Blackwell, Oxford: 1986) p 64.
8. Ramsden, *Making*, p 224.
9. Young, *Douglas-Home*, p 194.
10. *Wind Blows*, pp 78–9.
11. *Wind Blows*, p 77.
12. Hennessy, *Muddling Through*, p 243.
13. K O Morgan, *Labour People: Leaders and Lieutenants, Hardie to Kinnock* (Oxford University Press, Oxford: 1987) p 260.
14. P Ziegler, *Wilson: the Authorised Life of Lord Wilson of Rievaulx* (Weidenfeld and Nicolson, London: 1993) p 150.

15. A Clark, *The Tories: Conservatives and the Nation State 1922–1997* (Weidenfeld and Nicolson, London: 1998) p 332.

16. Sulzberger, *Giants*, p 1033.

17. Howard and West, *Making*, pp 85–6.

18. Gilmour and Garnett, *Whatever Happened*, p 187.

19. Thorpe, *Douglas-Home*, p 276.

20. Jefferys, *Retreat*, p 227.

21. H van Thal (ed), *The Prime Ministers: from Lord John Russell to Edward Heath* (Allen and Unwin, London: 1975) pp 368–9.

22. Thorpe, *Douglas-Home*, p 8.

23. Young, *Douglas-Home*, p 119.

24. Sulzberger, *Giants*, p 1037.

25. King, *Diary 1970–74*, p 280.

26. Young, *Douglas-Home*, p 4.

27. Hennessy, *Prime Minister*, p 285.

28. Earl of Swinton, *Sixty Years of Power: Some Memories of the Men who Wielded It* (Hutchinson, London: 1966) p 200.

29. W Douglas Home, *Mr Home pronounced Hume* (Collins, London: 1979) p 29.

30. Heffer, *Powell*, p 947.

31. Lord Carrington, *Reflect on Things Past: the Memoirs of Lord Carrington* (Collins, London: 1988) p 252.

32. J Margach, *The Abuse of Power: The War between Downing Street and the Media from Lloyd George to James Callaghan* (W H Allen, London: 1978) p 128.

33. P Rawlinson, *A Price Too High* (Weidenfeld and Nicolson, London: 1989) p 106.

34. Pimlott, *Queen*, p 324.

35. Cockerell, *Live from Number 10*, p 105.

36. Cockerell, *Live from Number 10*, p 107.

37. Hennessy, *Prime Minister*, p 284.

38. D Robertson, *A Theory of Party Competition* (Wiley, London: 1976) p 98.

39. *Wind Blows*, p 282.

40. D Rusk, *As I Saw It: a Secretary of State's Memoirs* (I B Tauris, London: 1991) pp 197–8.

41. Rusk, *As I Saw It*, p 197.

42. A Shlaim, P Jones and K Sainsbury, *British Foreign Secretaries since 1945* (David and Charles, Newton Abbot: 1977) p 149.

43. Young, *Douglas-Home*, p 191.

CHRONOLOGY

Year	Premiership

1963 19 October: Sir Alec Douglas-Home becomes Prime Minister, aged 60 and having renounced his title as 14th Earl of Home.
Gives dignified speech in Commons in memory of assassinated President Kennedy.

1964 Douglas-Home's tour to 'meet the people' is not a success.
Feb: Douglas-Home visits President Johnson in Washington
Abolition of Retail Price Maintenance.
Election campaign: Douglas-Home fares badly at public speaking, but begins to make up ground.
15 October: General election – Labour 317, Conservatives and allies 304.
16 October: Douglas-Home leaves office, having served three days short of one year.

History	Culture
President Kennedy is assassinated in Dallas, Texas by Lee Harvey Oswald. Lyndon B Johnson is sworn in as President.	John Le Carré, *The Spy Who Came in from the Cold*. Gerry and the Pacemakers, *You'll never walk alone.* The Beatles, *Please Please me.* Films: *The Great Escape. Cleopatra. Tom Jones.* TV: *Dr Who.*
Anti-US riots in Panama lead to breaking of diplomatic relations with USA. In South Africa, Nelson Mandela is sentenced to life imprisonment. Turkish planes attack Cyprus. UN orders cease-fire. Indonesian army lands in Malaya. Commonwealth troops move in. Khrushchev is replaced by Brezhnev as First Secretary of Soviet Communist Party. China explodes an atomic bomb.	Harnick/Bock, *Fiddler on the Roof.* Saul Bellow, *Herzog.* Philip Larkin, *The Whitsun Weddings.* Jean-Paul Sartre, *Les Mots.* Peter Shaffer, *The Royal Hunt of the Sun.* Films: *Mary Poppins. A Hard Day's Night.* TV: *Steptoe and Son. Crossroads. Top of the Pops. Match of the Day.* Radio: *Round the Horne.*

FURTHER READING

Though much less has been written specifically about Alec Douglas-Home than many other Prime Ministers of the 20th century, a substantial literature may be consulted with profit. The authorised biography by D R Thorpe, *Alec Douglas-Home* (Sinclair-Stevenson, London: 1996) is indispensable. It is the only work that has yet made significant use of Douglas-Home's private papers. Earlier biographies by John Dickie, *The Uncommon Commoner: a Study of Sir Alec Douglas-Home* (Pall Mall Press, London: 1964) and Kenneth Young, *Sir Alec Douglas-Home* (Dent, London: 1970) remain valuable, not least because the authors received significant co-operation from Douglas-Home himself.

Douglas-Home produced three books of his own. His memoirs, *The Way the Wind Blows* (Collins, London: 1976) disclose few political secrets, but offer revealing insights into the author's character. They are far removed from the turgid exercises in self-justification offered by many of Home's political contemporaries. *Letters to a Grandson* (Collins, London: 1983) is surprisingly informative about his views and beliefs, particularly relating to foreign affairs, while *Border Reflections: chiefly on the arts of shooting and fishing* (Collins, London: 1973) reveals his passion for wildlife, particularly killing it.

There are some interesting observations on Douglas-Home's early life in his brother's memoir, William Douglas Home, *Mr Home, Pronounced Hume* (Collins, London: 1979). Cyril Connolly's celebrated vignette of Eton at the time of the First World War is in *Enemies of Promise* (Penguin, Harmondsworth: 1961). Douglas-Home's early political career has left only fleeting impressions in the standard literature on the 1930s and 1940s, but Robert Rhodes James (ed), *Chips: the Diaries of Sir Henry Channon* (Weidenfeld and Nicolson, London: 1967) and John Colville, *The Fringes of Power: Downing Street Diaries 1939–1955* (Hodder, London: 1985) give some idea of his role in the entourage surrounding Neville Chamberlain. His work at the Scottish Office, 1951–5, is assessed in Anthony Seldon, *Churchill's Indian Summer* (Hodder and Stoughton, London: 1981), while his early Cabinet career may be traced in the works of Richard Lamb, *The Failure of the Eden Government* (Sidgwick and Jackson, London: 1987) and *The Macmillan Years 1957–1963: the Emerging Truth* (John Murray, London: 1995)

For the period after 1955 there is much valuable material in the biographies of and memoirs by Douglas-Home's political contemporaries. Among biographies see, in particular, Lewis Baston, *Reggie: the Life of Reginald Maudling* (Sutton, Stroud: 2004); John Campbell, *Edward Heath: a Biography* (Cape, London: 1993); David Dutton, *Anthony Eden: a Life and Reputation* (Arnold, London: 1997); Simon Heffer, *Like the Roman: the Life of Enoch Powell* (Weidenfeld and Nicolson, London: 1998); Alistair Horne, *Macmillan 1957–1986* (Macmillan, London: 1989); Anthony Howard, *RAB: the Life of R A Butler* (Cape, London: 1987); George Hutchinson, *The Last Edwardian at No 10* (Grafton, London: 1980) – particularly useful as it reprints Iain Macleod's *Spectator* polemic on the 1963 leadership contest; Geoffrey Lewis, *Lord Hailsham* (Cape, London: 1997); Ben Pimlott, *The Queen: a biography of Elizabeth II* (Harper Collins, London: 1997); Robert Shepherd, *Iain Macleod* (Hutchinson London: 1994); Robert Shepherd, *Enoch Powell* (Hutchinson, London: 1996); D R Thorpe, *Selwyn Lloyd* (Cape, London: 1989); Philip Ziegler, *Harold Wilson: the authorised biography* (Weidenfeld and Nicolson, London: 1993).

The more useful memoirs include Reginald Bevins, *The Greasy Pole* (Hodder, London: 1965); John Boyd-Carpenter, *Way of Life* (Sidgwick and Jackson, London: 1980); Lord Butler, *The Art of the Possible* (Penguin, Harmondsworth: 1973); Andrei Gromyko, *Memoirs* (Hutchinson, London: 1989); Lord Hailsham, *A Sparrow's Flight* (Collins, London: 1990); Edward Heath, *The Course of my Life* (Hodder and Stoughton, London: 1998); Harold Macmillan, *Riding the Storm 1956–1959*, *Pointing the Way 1959–1961* and *At the End of the Day 1961–1963* (Macmillan, London: 1971, 1972, 1973); Reginald Maudling, *Memoirs* (Sidgwick and Jackson, London: 1978); Earl of Swinton, *Sixty Years of Power* (Hutchinson, London: 1966); Roy Welensky, *Welensky's 4000 Days* (Collins, London: 1964). Note should also be made of four published diaries: Tony Benn, *Out of the Wilderness: Diaries 1963–67* (Hutchinson, London: 1987); Harold Evans, *Downing Street Diary: the Macmillan Years 1957–1963* (Hodder, London: 1981); Cecil King, *The Cecil King Diary 1970–1974* (Cape, London: 1975); and C L Sulzberger, *The Last of the Giants* (Weidenfeld and Nicolson, London: 1972).

For the context of Conservative Party politics John Ramsden, *The Winds of Change: Macmillan to Heath 1957–1975* (Longman, London: 1996) is indispensable. Ian Gilmour and Mark Garnett, *Whatever Happened to the Tories: the Conservative Party since 1945* (Fourth Estate, London: 1997) offers an insider's view. For the 1964 general election see David Butler and Anthony King, *The British General Election of 1964* (Macmillan, London: 1965). Anthony Howard and Richard West, *The Making of the Prime Minister* (Cape, London: 1965) is also useful. Randolph Churchill's *The Fight for the Tory Leadership: a Contemporary Chronicle* (Heinemann, London: 1964) should be treated with caution. The works of Peter Hennessy are full of illuminating information and ideas. See, in particular, *The Prime Minister: the Office and its Holders since 1945* (Penguin, London: 2001).

For Douglas-Home's performance as Foreign Secretary, reference should be made to A Shlaim, P Jones and K Sainsbury, *British Foreign Secretaries since 1945* (David and Charles, Newton Abbot: 1977); J P S Gearson, *Harold Macmillan and the Berlin Wall Crisis, 1958–62* (Macmillan, Basingstoke: 1998); A James, *Britain and the Congo Crisis 1960–1963* (Macmillan, Basingstoke: 1996); Kendrick Oliver, *Kennedy, Macmillan and the Nuclear Test-Ban Debate 1961–63* (Macmillan, Basingstoke: 1998). Andrew Holt, 'Lord Home and Anglo-American Relations, 1961–1963', *Diplomacy and Statecraft* 16 (2005) offers a very recent re-assessment.

PICTURE SOURCES

Pages 8–9
In his retirement Sir Alec Douglas-Home is photographed at his home in Scotland, 18 March 1979. (Courtesy Topham Picturepoint)

Page 61
The Prime Minister Sir Alec Douglas-Home addresses the fourth Young Conservatives National Conference, 15 February 1964. (Courtesy Topham Picturepoint)

Page 125
After his premiership the MP for Kinross and West Perthshire Sir Alec Douglas-Home and his wife Lady Elizabeth. (Courtesy Topham Picturepoint)

INDEX

A

Adenauer, Konrad 36
Aitken, William Maxwell 7
Alington, Elizabeth (wife)
    16, 108
Allen, G O 5
Amery, Julian 50
Amery, Leo 9
Anstruther-Gray, William
    51, 92
Asquith, Herbert Henry
    123
Attlee, Clement 16, 46, 67,
    74, 78, 121

B

Baldwin, Stanley 8, 77, 87,
    117
Balfour, Arthur 1, 87, 93
Banda, Hastings 28
Barber, Anthony 64
Beaverbrook, Lord 6
Beckett, Clare 107
Beckett, Francis 25
Benn, Tony 63, 65, 68
Bevins, Reginald 55, 114
Blair, Tony 46, 73, 107
Blakenham, Lord 81

Bloom, John 81
Bonar Law, Andrew 69,
    109
Boyd-Carpenter, John 54,
    57, 92
Boyle, Sir Edward 55, 57
Bracken, Brendan 12
Brandt, Willy 101
Brown, George 66, 81,
    82
Burton, Montagu 113
Bush, George W 73
Butler, R A 23, 42, 46 ff.,
    51 ff., 53, 54, 55 ff., 58
    ff., 63, 71, 82, 83 ff., 89,
    107

C

Callaghan, James 76, 105,
    118
Cameron, David 50
Cameron, James 63
Carr, Robert 104
Carrington, Peter 97, 118
Chamberlain, Neville 8 ff.,
    14, 49, 71, 97
Chelmer, Lord 54
Churchill, Randolph 32

THE 20 BRITISH PRIME MINISTERS
OF THE 20TH CENTURY

Salisbury

SALISBURY
Conservative politician, prime minister
1885–6, 1886–92 and 1895–1902, and
the last to hold that office in the House
of Lords.
by Eric Midwinter
Visiting Professor of Education at
Exeter University
ISBN 1-904950-54-X (pb)

Balfour

BALFOUR
Balfour wrote that Britain favoured 'the
establishment in Palestine of a national
home for the Jewish people', the so-
called 'Balfour Declaration'.
by Ewen Green
of Magdalen College Oxford
ISBN 1-904950-55-8 (pb)

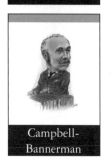

Campbell-
Bannerman

CAMPBELL-BANNERMAN
Liberal Prime Minister, who started the
battle with the Conservative-dominated
House of Lords.
by Lord Hattersley
former Deputy Leader of the Labour
Party and Cabinet member in Wilson
and Callaghan's governments.
ISBN 1-904950-56-6 (pb)

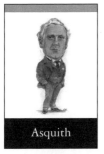

Asquith

ASQUITH

His administration laid the foundation of Britain's welfare state, but he was plunged into a major power struggle with the House of Lords.

by Stephen Bates

a senior correspondent for the *Guardian*.

ISBN 1-904950-57-4 (pb)

Lloyd George

LLOYD GEORGE

By the end of 1916 there was discontent with Asquith's management of the war, and Lloyd George schemed secretly with the Conservatives in the coalition government to take his place.

by Hugh Purcell

television documentary maker.

ISBN 1-904950-58-2 (pb)

Bonar Law

BONAR LAW

In 1922 he was the moving spirit in the stormy meeting of Conservative MPs which ended the coalition, created the 1922 Committee and reinstated him as leader.

by Andrew Taylor

Professor of Politics at the University of Sheffield.

ISBN 1-904950-59-0 (pb)

Baldwin

BALDWIN

Baldwin's terms of office included two major political crises, the General Strike and the Abdication.

by Anne Perkins

a journalist, working mostly for the *Guardian*, as well as a historian of the British labour movement.

ISBN 1-904950-60-4 (pb)

MACDONALD

In 1900 he was the first secretary of the newly formed Labour Representation Committee (the original name for the Labour party). Four years later he became the first Labour prime minister.

by Kevin Morgan

who teaches government and politics at Manchester University.
ISBN 1-904950-61-2 (pb)

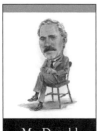

MacDonald

CHAMBERLAIN

His name will forever be linked to the policy of appeasement and the Munich agreement he reached with Hitler.

by Graham Macklin

manager of the research service at the National Archives.
ISBN 1-904950-62-0 (pb)

Chamberlain

CHURCHILL

Perhaps the most determined and inspirational war leader in Britain's history.

by Chris Wrigley

who has written about David Lloyd George, Arthur Henderson and W E Gladstone.
ISBN 1-904950-63-9 (pb)

Churchill

ATTLEE

His post-war government enacted a broad programme of socialist legislation in spite of conditions of austerity. His legacy: the National Health Service.

by David Howell

Professor of Politics at the University of York and an expert in Labour's history.
ISBN 1-904950-64-7 (pb)

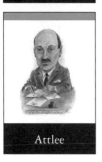

Attlee

Eden

EDEN
His premiership will forever be linked to the
fateful Suez Crisis.
by Peter Wilby
former editor of the *New Statesman*.
ISBN 1-904950-65-5 (pb)

Macmillan

MACMILLAN
He repaired the rift between the USA and
Britain created by Suez and secured for Britain
co-operation on issues of nuclear defence, but
entry into the EEC was vetoed by de Gaulle in
1963.
by Francis Beckett
author of BEVAN, published by Haus in
2004.
ISBN 1-904950-66-3 (pb)

Douglas-Home

DOUGLAS-HOME
Conservative politician and prime minister
1963-4, with a complex career between the
two Houses of Parliament.
by David Dutton
who teaches History at Liverpool
University.
ISBN 1-904950-67-1 (pb)

Wilson

WILSON
He held out the promise progress, of 'the
Britain that is going to be forged in the white
heat of this revolution'. The forced devaluation
of the pound in 1967 frustrated the fulfilment
of his promises.
by Paul Routledge
The *Daily Mirror's* chief political
commentator.
ISBN 1-904950-68-X (pb)

Heath

HEATH

A passionate European, he succeeded during his premiership in effecting Britain's entry to the EC.

by Denis MacShane

Minister for Europe in Tony Blair's first government.

ISBN 1-904950-69-8 (pb)

Callaghan

CALLAGHAN

His term in office was dominated by industrial unrest, culminating in the 'Winter of Discontent'.

by Harry Conroy

When James Callaghan was Prime Minister, Conroy was the Labour Party's press officer in Scotland, and he is now editor of the Scottish *Catholic Observer.*

ISBN 1-904950-70-1 (pb)

Thatcher

THATCHER

Britain's first woman prime minister and the longest serving head of government in the 20th century (1979–90), but also the only one to be removed from office in peacetime by pressure from within her own party.

by Clare Beckett

teaches social policy at Bradford University.

ISBN 1-904950-71-X (pb)

Major

MAJOR

He enjoyed great popularity in his early months as prime minister, as he seemed more caring than his iron predecessor, but by the end of 1992 nothing seemed to go right.

by Robert Taylor

is Research Associate at the LSE's Centre for Economic Performance.

ISBN 1-904950-72-8 (pb)

Blair

BLAIR

He is therefore the last prime minister of the 20th century and one of the most controversial ones, being frequently accused of abandoning cabinet government and introducing a presidential style of leadership.

by Mick Temple

is a senior lecturer in Politics and Journalism at Staffordshire University.

ISBN 1-904950-73-6 (pb)

THE 20 BRITISH PRIME MINISTERS
OF THE 20TH CENTURY

www.hauspublishing.co.uk

MAO
by Nigel Jones
ISBN 1-904341-09-8 (pb)

The life of the peasant farmer's son who became ruler of the world's most populous nation is one of the most remarkable stories of the 20th century. His leadership of the communist revolution and the establishment of the People's Republic of China in 1949, after two decades of civil war and Japanese invasion, earned him the title of Chairman Mao. Alternately glorified and demonised, not only in the West but also in the China he once ruled, his influence persists to this day.

Jonathan Clements' excellent biography capitalises on new information to tell this remarkable story. He shows how Mao's outdated Confucian education left him resentful of those with modern knowledge and experience of languages and cultures beyond China. How his wilful ignorance of foreign matters and determination to try and defeat any challenge, sowed the seeds of many flawed political decisions and national disasters.

Millions of Chinese people died during the Cultural Revolution 40 years ago, yet he still remains an iconic figure and his influence persists to this day. China is now the single largest market for capitalist products in the world and as Jonathan Clements points out, it is ironic that Mao's picture appears on everything from blankets to Chinese banknotes.